cooking
desserts

cooking
desserts

Katy Holder

THUNDER BAY
P · R · E · S · S

San Diego, California

contents

a taste for all seasons

Many cookbooks explore exotic corners of the culinary world or delight in extending skills and knowledge. This book, however, has a very simple aim: to offer great desserts that work every time. The chosen recipes are not tricky or fancy; they are all reliable, a few even very simple, and many are welcomingly familiar. Above all, they taste, smell, and look wonderful. They are divided by season, with an emphasis on fresh, good-quality ingredients and classic dessert-making techniques. If you glance through the book's pages, moving from one season to another, you'll discover desserts so tempting that you will wish it were summer, autumn, winter, and spring all at the same time so that you could delve into everything right away! Even the names sound good— brown sugar cream pots with roasted plums in autumn; coconut, mango, and almond pie in spring; mango and star anise sorbet for summer; and decadent chocolate and cinnamon self-saucing puddings in winter.

Fruits are central to many recipes and have been largely kept to their season— so you won't see fresh figs in a spring recipe or blueberries in the winter chapter. You will be well rewarded if you can wait for summer to arrive before indulging in strawberry and mascarpone mousse or the onset of cold, short days to savor some pear and walnut frangipane pie. The basic building blocks of cakes, pastries, and puddings—eggs, flour, sugar, butter, cream, and vanilla—are common to all chapters, and with these on hand you often only need to buy a few more ingredients and you are on your way. Add some fruit, chocolate, honey, nuts, liqueurs, or spices such as cardamom and cinnamon for some truly memorable desserts.

A number of essential techniques are covered—classic procedures that you will come across time and time again and so are good to master. These include how to make perfect pie pastry, custard, and glossy meringue. Some recipes are demanding, but that can be exactly what you're looking for every now and then. Try profiteroles with coffee mascarpone and bittersweet chocolate sauce in spring or chocolate ganache log in autumn when you feel like a challenge. Many other recipes are almost suspiciously simple. Also, like with the ingredients, you may find that most of the necessary equipment is already in your kitchen, such as a food processor and blender, cake pans of various sizes, sieves, bowls, spoons, and rolling pins.

Nothing will entice you more than the desserts themselves, which really need no introduction.

spring

Pretty colors and gentle flavors characterize the desserts in this chapter. For example, cardamom kulfi and delicate panna cotta phyllo with rosewater syrup and pistachios could only be delightful spring treats. The dishes are not yet filled with the brilliance and boldness of summer flavors but at the same time are no longer dominated by the rich heaviness of winter ingredients. Many contain a bit of both—lime and coconut rice pudding, for example, retains the comforting texture of a winter dish but marks the new season with the clean taste of lime and even looks forward to the summer months with creamy tropical coconut.

As there should be when spring arrives, there is a lightness and freshness to these desserts. There is even an element of healthiness to them—but not too much!—with the clean, tart, citrus flavors of limes and lemons; the slight sharpness of yogurt; and the tang of ginger to give things a little bite and wake up the taste buds. Refreshing granitas and gelati in shades of ruby red and pale gold start to make an appearance, as do fruit-filled pies and light pastries. Baked desserts like lemon pie and lemon, fig, and walnut cake are a sure sign that afternoons can be reclaimed from the slumber of winter.

Chocolate and alcohol don't feature highly, but lest you fear a too-healthy shock to the system, there are still desserts with a good dash of cream of one sort or another in them—chocolate almondine semifreddo is nothing if not indulgent—and there are a few desserts that keep chocolate close by as a sauce that you can add as generously as you like.

Of the classic techniques introduced in this chapter, perhaps the most difficult would be making perfectly smooth custard for the coconut and ginger crème brûlée. The trick is to ensure that the water in the bain-marie does not bubble or bubbles will form in the custard. This is more of a concern when making crème caramel, as you can see the bubbles in the custard when you turn it out, but it is still worth getting the technique right when making a crème brûlée. On the other hand, no one is going to turn away a rich, gooey custard just because of a few bubbles, so relax.

coconut and ginger crème brûlée

THIS TRADITIONAL BAKED EGG CUSTARD IS GIVEN A TOUCH OF THE TROPICAL THROUGH THE ADDITION OF GINGER AND COCONUT—ALL THE MORE PLEASANT BECAUSE THEIR SHARP, FRESH FLAVORS ARE UNEXPECTED. DON'T RUSH THIS RECIPE—IT'S NOT COMPLICATED, BUT EACH STEP NEEDS TO BE FOLLOWED WITH CARE.

light cream	2 cups
shredded dried coconut	1/3 cup
fresh ginger	3 teaspoons finely grated
egg yolks	4, at room temperature
superfine sugar	1/4 cup
raw sugar	2 tablespoons

Preheat the oven to 315°F.

Put the cream, shredded dried coconut, and ginger into a saucepan. Slowly heat the mixture, stirring, until it is just below boiling point. Strain into a bowl, discarding the coconut and ginger.

Whisk the egg yolks and superfine sugar in a heatproof bowl until thick and pale. This will take about 5 minutes with an electric whisk. Gradually whisk in the hot cream. Place the bowl over a saucepan of barely simmering water, making sure the base of the bowl doesn't touch the water. Stir the mixture over the simmering water for 10 minutes, or until it has thickened slightly and coats the back of a spoon.

Put four 1/2-cup capacity ovenproof dishes in a roasting pan and divide the cream mixture among the dishes. Add enough boiling water to the roasting pan to come three-quarters of the way up the side of the dishes. Bake for 20–25 minutes, or until the custards are just set. Carefully remove the dishes from the water and set aside to cool to room temperature, then cover and refrigerate the custards for 3 hours.

Preheat the broiler to high. Put the custards in a shallow roasting pan and surround them with ice cubes. Sprinkle the tops of the custards with the raw sugar. Place under the hot broiler until the sugar has melted and turned golden brown. Alternatively, use a small blowtorch to caramelize the sugar.

Whisk the egg yolks and super-fine sugar until thick and pale.

The custard must be thick enough to coat the back of the spoon.

ruby-red grapefruit granita.......................serves 4–6

GRANITA CAN BE MADE FROM ANY CITRUS FRUIT—LEMON IS THE CLASSIC CHOICE, BUT GRAPEFRUIT, ORANGE, AND LIME CAN ALL BE USED SUCCESSFULLY. TANGY AND SMOOTH AT THE SAME TIME, THIS PRETTY RUBY-RED VERSION LITERALLY MELTS IN THE MOUTH. YOU WILL NEED ABOUT THREE GRAPEFRUIT FOR THIS RECIPE.

sugar	1/2 cup
freshly squeezed ruby-red grapefruit juice	1 1/2 cups
orange muscat dessert wine	2/3 cup

Put the sugar and 1/2 cup of water in a small saucepan and bring to a boil. Reduce the heat and simmer for 3–4 minutes, then remove from heat and set aside to cool.

Combine the grapefruit juice, wine, and sugar syrup in a shallow freezer-proof tray and freeze for 2 hours, or until the mixture has started to freeze around the edges. Break up the mixture with a fork, then return it to the freezer and repeat the process every 30 minutes until the granita has frozen and has a rough, icy texture.

Grapefruit arrived relatively recently on the culinary scene, first introduced into North America from the Bahamas in the early nineteenth century. Today, they are available with or without seeds and in a range of colors, from yellow to pink to ruby-red. The original yellow-fleshed fruit is a favorite for breakfast; eaten fresh, with maybe just a sprinkling of sugar, it makes a fairly bracing start to the day. The pinker varieties are generally sweeter. Grapefruit go well with cheese, pears, and certain nuts, they make good marmalade, and they are delicious in chicken and shrimp salads, fruit salads, sorbets, and granitas. Choose heavy fruit with unblemished skin.

panna cotta phyllo with rosewater syrup and pistachios.....................serves 6

THIS RECIPE SEEMS COMPLICATED, BUT ONCE THE PANNA COTTA IS MADE AND SAFELY IN THE REFRIGERATOR, IT'S ALL SMOOTH SAILING. TAKE CARE TO ADD ONLY THE SPECIFIED AMOUNT OF ROSE WATER, SINCE IT CAN BE SURPRISINGLY STRONG——TOO MUCH AND THE SYRUP WILL BE SICKLY SWEET.

panna cotta

gelatin	half of a $1/4$-ounce envelope, or $1 1/2$ teaspoons powdered
light cream	2 cups
plain yogurt	1 cup
superfine sugar	$2/3$ cup
vanilla bean	1

phyllo shells

phyllo pastry	4 sheets
unsalted butter	3 tablespoons, melted
superfine sugar	2 tablespoons

rosewater syrup

superfine sugar	$1/2$ cup
cinnamon stick	1
rose water	$1/2$ teaspoon
rose-pink food coloring	1 drop, optional
roasted pistachio nuts	2 tablespoons, chopped

To make the panna cotta, put 2 tablespoons of water in a small bowl, sprinkle with the gelatin, and set aside for 2 minutes to sponge and swell. Put the cream, yogurt, and sugar in a saucepan. Spilt the vanilla bean lengthwise and scrape the seeds into the saucepan, discarding the pod. Stir the mixture over low heat until the sugar has dissolved. Add the sponged gelatin to the saucepan and stir until the gelatin has dissolved. Pour the mixture into six $1/2$-cup molds. Refrigerate for 5 hours, or until set.

Meanwhile, preheat the oven to 375°F. Lightly brush a sheet of phyllo pastry with the melted butter. Sprinkle one-third of the sugar over the pastry, top with another sheet of pastry, and press down gently to stick the pastry together. Repeat this process until there are four layers of pastry. Using a sharp knife, cut six $4 1/2$-inch square pieces from the pastry. Line a six-hole, giant muffin pan with the pastry squares. Line each pastry shell with a square of baking paper and weigh it down with baking beads or uncooked rice. Bake for 2 minutes, then remove the paper and beads and bake for a further 2–3 minutes, or until lightly golden. Cool the pastry shells on a wire rack.

To make the rosewater syrup, put $2/3$ cup water, the sugar, and cinnamon stick in a small saucepan. Stir over low heat until the sugar has dissolved. Increase the heat to high and simmer for 3–4 minutes, or until the mixture is slightly syrupy. Add the rose water and food coloring, if using. Remove from heat and set aside to cool. Remove the cinnamon stick.

Run a spatula or blunt knife around the panna cotta, then carefully invert them into the pastry shells. Drizzle the panna cotta with the rosewater syrup and sprinkle with the pistachios.

Make sure you use a muffin pan with large holes.

Simmer the rosewater syrup until it is slightly syrupy.

cardamom kulfi ....serves 8

THIS SIMPLE, ELEGANT ICE CREAM FROM INDIA IS MADE BY BOILING MILK UNTIL IT REDUCES AND CONDENSES, THEN FLAVORING IT WITH INGREDIENTS SUCH AS PISTACHIO NUTS, CARDAMOM, AND ROSE WATER. TO TURN OUT THE KULFI, BRIEFLY DIP THE MOLDS IN VERY HOT WATER, THEN INVERT THEM ONTO SERVING PLATES.

pistachio nuts	1/4 cup
milk	6 cups
cardamom pods	21
superfine sugar	1/2 cup
lime zest	1/2 teaspoon finely grated

Preheat the broiler to medium. Spread the pistachios on a baking sheet and place under the broiler for about 3 minutes, or until aromatic and lightly toasted. Set aside to cool slightly, then roughly chop the nuts.

Put the milk and 9 of the cardamom pods in a large, heavy-based saucepan. Bring to a boil, making sure the milk doesn't boil over. Reduce heat and simmer for 15–20 minutes, or until the liquid has reduced by one-third. Strain the mixture into a container suitable for freezing. Add the sugar and stir until it has dissolved. Stir in half the chopped pistachios and the grated lime zest. Set aside to cool for 30 minutes. Store the remaining pistachios in an airtight container.

Freeze the kulfi until almost firm, stirring every 30 minutes. (This can take from 3 to 6 hours, depending on the freezer.) Rinse eight 2/3-cup dariole molds with cold water and shake out the excess. Pack the kulfi into the molds and freeze until completely firm.

Remove the molds from the freezer 5 minutes before serving. Turn the kulfi out onto serving plates and sprinkle the reserved pistachios over the top. Lightly crush the remaining cardamom pods to release some of the seeds. Sprinkle a few seeds on top of the kulfi, and sprinkle the pods around the base.

Strain the milk to remove the cardamom pods.

Add half the chopped pistachios and all the grated lime zest.

Once the kulfi is almost firm, pack it into dariole molds.

banana and pineapple tortilla fingers

BANANA FRITTERS ARE COMMONLY MADE WITH BATTER, DEEP-FRIED, AND THEN SERVED PIPING HOT WITH ICE CREAM OR COCONUT CREAM. THIS VERSION MAKES LIFE EASY BY USING TORTILLAS AND BROILING RATHER THAN FRYING THE FRITTERS, WHILE THE PINEAPPLE ADDS A JUICY, SWEET, CARAMELIZED FLAVOR.

fresh pineapple	4 thin slices
white, wheat flour tortillas	4 large
bananas	2
unsalted butter	3 tablespoons, melted
confectioners' sugar	for dusting

coconut yogurt

plain yogurt	1/2 cup
soft brown sugar	1/3 cup
shredded dried coconut	2 tablespoons
lemon zest	2 teaspoons finely grated
lemon juice	1 teaspoon

Preheat the broiler to high. Cut each pineapple slice into thirds and remove the hard core. Broil the pineapple for 8 minutes each side, or until just starting to brown. Remove and set aside to cool.

To make the coconut yogurt, put the yogurt, half the brown sugar, the shredded dried coconut, lemon zest, and lemon juice in a small bowl and stir to combine. Refrigerate until needed.

Cut the tortillas into three even strips, each about 2 inches wide. Peel the bananas and cut them in half lengthwise and then into pieces slightly longer than the width of the tortilla strips. Roll the banana pieces in half of the melted butter and sprinkle with the remaining brown sugar. Place a piece of pineapple widthwise across the center of each tortilla strip and top with a piece of banana. Fold the tortilla over the banana, roll up, and place on a baking sheet, seam side down. Brush the tortillas with the remaining melted butter.

Preheat the broiler to high. Broil the tortilla fingers for 8–10 minutes, or until golden brown, then turn and cook until browned all over. Dust with confectioners' sugar and serve with the coconut yogurt.

Cut each of the tortillas into three even strips.

Place the pineapple and banana widthwise across the tortillas.

Carefully roll up the tortillas to enclose the filling.

white chocolate mousse with almond tuiles . . . . serves 6

TRYING A NEW RECIPE CAN BE REWARDING, AND IT'S PERHAPS NORMAL THAT WE SET CULINARY CHALLENGES FOR OURSELVES PRECISELY WHEN WE SHOULDN'T—THAT IS, WHEN GUESTS ARE COMING FOR DINNER. THIS DESSERT IS A GOOD CHOICE FOR SUCH OCCASIONS SINCE IT NOT ONLY LOOKS IMPRESSIVE BUT ALSO CAN BE MADE IN ADVANCE.

egg yolks	6, at room temperature
superfine sugar	1/4 cup
milk	1 1/2 cups
white chocolate chips	1 1/4 cups
cognac	1/3 cup
powdered gelatin	2 teaspoons
light cream	1 3/4 cups

almond tuiles

light corn syrup	1 tablespoon
unsalted butter	2 tablespoons
raw superfine sugar	1 1/2 tablespoons
all-purpose flour	2 tablespoons
blanched almonds	scant 1/4 cup, finely chopped

Beat the egg yolks and superfine sugar in a bowl until smooth and pale. This will take about 5 minutes with an electric whisk. Pour the milk into a saucepan and heat until it is just below the boiling point. Whisk the hot milk into the egg yolk mixture, then return the mixture to the saucepan. Cook over low heat, stirring constantly, for about 2 minutes, or until the mixture is thick enough to coat the back of a spoon. Do not allow the mixture to boil or it will separate.

Strain the mixture into a bowl, add the white chocolate chips, and stir until the chocolate has melted. Stir in the cognac. Put 1 1/2 tablespoons of water in a small bowl and sprinkle with the gelatin. Leave the gelatin to sponge and swell. Stir the gelatin mixture into the chocolate mixture and set aside to cool for at least 1 hour.

Whip the cream until soft peaks form. Using a metal spoon, fold a large scoop of cream into the chocolate mixture, then gently fold in the remaining cream. Divide the mixture among six 3/4-cup glasses and refrigerate until set.

Meanwhile, to make the almond tuiles, preheat the oven to 350°F. Line a cookie sheet with baking paper. Put the corn syrup, butter, and sugar in a saucepan and cook over low heat, stirring until melted. Increase the heat and bring to a boil. Immediately remove the saucepan from the heat and stir in the flour and almonds.

Using half the mixture, spoon teaspoons of it onto the prepared sheet, allowing for spreading. Bake for 4–5 minutes, or until golden brown. Set aside to cool for 15–20 seconds, then, using a spatula and working quickly, lift the cookies and drape them over a rolling pin or the handle of a wooden spoon. They will quickly set in a curved shape. Repeat with the remaining mixture. Store the tuiles in an airtight container until ready to serve.

Serve the mousse with the almond tuiles.

lime and coconut rice puddings

IT'S NO ACCIDENT THAT LIMES AND COCONUTS GROW IN SIMILAR PARTS OF THE WORLD: THEIR FLAVORS COMPLEMENT EACH OTHER PERFECTLY. THE SHARPNESS OF LIME MEANS IT IS OFTEN USED AS A FLAVOR ENHANCER, AND HERE IT NICELY CUTS THROUGH THE RICHNESS OF THE COCONUT CREAM.

milk	¾ cup
unsweetened coconut cream	3 cups
lime zest	of 1 lime, finely grated
lime juice	¼ cup
Kaffir lime leaves	3, halved
medium-grain rice	⅔ cup
jaggery	¾ cup shaved (or ½ cup soft brown sugar)
toasted shredded coconut	for decoration, optional

Put the milk, coconut cream, lime zest, lime juice, and lime leaves in a large saucepan and bring to a boil. Add the rice and stir to combine. Reduce the heat to low and simmer, stirring occasionally, for 25–30 minutes, or until the rice is tender.

Remove the saucepan from the heat and add the jaggery or brown sugar, stirring until it has dissolved and the mixture is creamy.

Remove the lime leaves and divide the rice pudding among four, 1-cup-capacity, heatproof glasses or ramekins. Serve warm or cold, decorated with shredded coconut, if using.

The coconut tree and its fruit have been appreciated for centuries. Its uses range from supplying material for thatching and weaving to providing a nutritious and refreshing drink—complete with its own cup. When not quite ripe, coconut flesh is soft and jellylike and the juice sweet and watery. As the coconut ripens, the flesh hardens and the amount of juice decreases. This juice is quite different from coconut cream, which is produced by soaking grated coconut flesh in boiling water and squeezing out the resulting liquid. Other products include copra, which is dried coconut flesh; coconut oil, which is made from copra; shredded dried coconut; and coconut liqueur.

three ways with garnishes

THERE IS MORE TO GARNISHES THAN CHOCOLATE CURLS AND GLACÉ CHERRIES. YET THEY DON'T NEED TO BE FUSSY AND PAINSTAKING TO MAKE, EITHER, AS THE FOLLOWING IDEAS SHOW. WHEN MAKING THE PRALINE, TAKE CARE NOT TO LET THE SUGAR GO PAST A DEEP CARAMEL COLOR——HAVE A BOWL OF ICE WATER READY TO DIP THE SAUCEPAN IN IF NEED BE. THE PRALINE AND CANDIED WALNUTS CAN BE MADE IN ADVANCE AND STORED IN AIRTIGHT CONTAINERS; THE COCONUT TUILES ARE BEST MADE ON THE DAY OF SERVING.

hazelnut and vanilla praline

Coarsely chop 1/2 cup roasted, skinned hazelnuts and spread the nuts on a baking sheet lined with baking paper. Put 1 cup superfine sugar and 1/2 cup water into a small saucepan. Split a vanilla bean in half lengthwise and scrape the seeds into the saucepan, discarding the pod. Cook over low heat, stirring until the sugar has dissolved. Bring to a boil and, without stirring, cook for 5 minutes, or until the mixture turns a deep golden color. Pour the mixture over the hazelnuts and leave to set for 15 minutes. Break up the praline with your hands or crush it in a food processor and sprinkle it over ice cream or stir it into lightly whipped cream. Makes about 2 cups.

candied walnuts

Preheat the oven to 350°F. Combine 1 cup roasted walnut halves, 2 tablespoons raw sugar, and 2 tablespoons corn syrup in a bowl. Spread the mixture onto a baking sheet lined with baking paper and bake for 5 minutes. Remove from the oven and toss to mix everything well. Return to the oven and bake for another 5 minutes. Leave the walnuts to cool on the sheet, then remove them with a spatula. Use the walnuts in cookie dough, to decorate cakes and pies, or stir them into softened vanilla ice cream and freeze until firm. Makes 1 cup.

coconut tuiles

Preheat the oven to 350°F. Combine 1/4 cup superfine sugar, 1/3 cup shredded dried coconut, and 2 teaspoons all-purpose flour in a bowl. Add 1 lightly beaten egg white and 2 teaspoons melted unsalted butter, and stir to combine. Drop 1/2 teaspoon of the mixture onto a baking sheet lined with baking paper. Using the back of a teaspoon dipped in water, spread out the mixture to a very thin 4-inch circle, leaving 2 inches between each tuile. Repeat with the remaining mixture. Bake for 5 minutes, or until lightly golden. Leave the cookies on the sheets to cool. These tuiles are great as a garnish for cold desserts and ice cream. Makes 20.

hazelnut and vanilla praline

coconut, mango, and almond pie .... serves 6–8

WHEN YOU HAVE A LOVELY, RIPE MANGO ON HAND, IT'S HARD NOT TO JUST EAT IT RIGHT THEN AND THERE AND FORGET THE DESSERT. BUT MANGO AND ALMONDS IN BUTTERY PASTRY IS A CLASSIC COMBINATION AND WORTH THE TEMPORARY EFFORT OF SELF-RESTRAINT. THE ALMOND PASTRY SHOULD BE CHILLED WELL BEFORE USING.

pastry

all-purpose flour	1$2/3$ cups
raw superfine sugar	1/4 cup
ground almonds	1/4 cup
unsalted butter	3/4 cup, chilled and cubed
egg yolks	2, at room temperature
ice water	1–2 tablespoons

filling

unsalted butter	3/4 cup, softened
raw superfine sugar	heaping 3/4 cup
eggs	2, at room temperature
ground almonds	2/3 cup
all-purpose flour	1/2 cup
shredded dried coconut	1 cup
unsweetened coconut cream	2 tablespoons
coconut liqueur	1 tablespoon
mango	1
flaked coconut	1/2 cup
vanilla ice cream, or whipped cream	to serve

To make the pastry, put the flour, sugar, ground almonds, and butter in a food processor. Process until the mixture resembles fine crumbs. Add the egg yolks and process until smooth. Add the water, 1/2 teaspoon at a time, until the dough clumps together in a ball. Flatten the dough to a rough rectangle, cover with plastic wrap, and refrigerate for 30 minutes.

Preheat the oven to 375°F. Grease a 7 x 11-inch loose-bottom pie pan.

To make the filling, cream the butter and sugar with an electric beater for about 3 minutes. Add the eggs, one at a time, beating well after each addition. Fold in the ground almonds, flour, and shredded dried coconut. Lightly stir in the coconut cream and coconut liqueur.

Roll out the pastry on a sheet of baking paper to cover the base and side of the pan. Place the pastry in the pan and trim any excess. Line the pastry with a sheet of crumpled baking paper and pour in some baking beads or uncooked rice. Bake for 10 minutes, remove the paper and beads, and bake for another 5 minutes. Reduce the oven to 325°F.

Cut the cheeks from the mango, peel them, and cut each into 1/8-inch thick slices. Spread the filling in the pastry case and arrange the mango slices in two rows down the length of the filling. Sprinkle the flaked coconut over the top and press it into the exposed filling with your fingertips, giving an uneven surface. Bake for 30 minutes, or until the coconut begins to brown, then cover loosely with foil. Bake for another 35 minutes, or until the filling is set and the top is golden brown. Serve warm with vanilla ice cream or serve cold with lightly whipped cream.

Arrange the mango slices in two rows over the filling.

The flaked coconut doesn't have to be arranged neatly.

ginger and grapefruit pudding
with mascarpone cream .... serves 6

THIS PUDDING IS IDEAL FOR SPRING, WHEN ANYTHING TOO HEAVY OR RICH DOESN'T FEEL RIGHT. IT HAS A LIGHT, CLEAN FLAVOR DUE TO THE GINGER AND RUBY-RED GRAPEFRUIT, WHICH IS MATCHED BY A FLUFFY, WARM SPONGE CAKE. OF COURSE, IF THAT SOUNDS TOO HEALTHY, YOU CAN ADD A GOOD DOLLOP OF MASCARPONE.

ruby-red grapefruit	1 large
crystallized ginger in syrup	1/3 cup drained
	plus 3 teaspoons syrup
dark corn syrup	1 1/2 tablespoons
unsalted butter	1/2 cup, softened
superfine sugar	1/2 cup
eggs	2, at room temperature
self-rising flour	1 1/2 cups
ground ginger	1 teaspoon
milk	1/3 cup

mascarpone cream

mascarpone cheese	heaping 1/2 cup
light cream	1/2 cup
confectioners' sugar	1 tablespoon, sifted

Preheat the oven to 325°F. Grease six 2/3-cup molds or ramekins.

Finely grate 2 teaspoons of zest from the grapefruit and set aside. Slice the grapefruit around its circumference, one-third of the way down. Peel the larger piece of grapefruit, removing any white pith, and cut the flesh into six 1/2-inch slices. Squeeze 3 teaspoons of juice from the remaining grapefruit. Finely chop the crystallized ginger and set aside.

Combine the grapefruit juice, ginger syrup, and corn syrup in a small bowl. Divide the mixture among the molds and top with a slice of grapefruit, trimming to fit.

Put the butter and sugar in a bowl and beat with an electric beater until pale and smooth. Beat in the eggs, one at a time. Sift in the flour and ground ginger, add the grapefruit zest, chopped ginger, and milk, and mix well. Divide the mixture among the molds.

Cover each mold with foil and put them in a deep roasting pan. Pour in enough boiling water to come halfway up the side of the molds. Cover the roasting pan with foil, sealing the edges well. Bake the desserts for 30–35 minutes, or until set.

To make the mascarpone cream, mix the mascarpone, cream, and confectioners' sugar in a small bowl until smooth.

To serve, gently invert the desserts onto serving plates and serve with the mascarpone cream.

The grapefruit syrup gives the puddings a lovely moist top.

Use scissors to trim the grapefruit to fit the molds.

limoncello syllabub . . . . serves 6

THIS ELEGANT DESSERT HAS ITS ORIGINS IN THE BRITISH COUNTRYSIDE OF THE SEVENTEENTH CENTURY, THOUGH THE ADDITION OF LIMONCELLO GIVES THE SYLLABUB A DEFINITE FEELING OF SOUTHERN ITALY. DON'T OMIT THE ALMOND TUILE COOKIES, AS THEY PROVIDE A CRISP CONTRAST TO THE SYLLABUB'S LIGHT AND CREAMY TEXTURE.

limoncello	½ cup
superfine sugar	½ cup
lemon zest	1 teaspoon finely grated
lemon juice	¼ cup
vanilla bean	1
light cream	1 cup
almond tuile cookies	to serve (page 23)

Put the limoncello in a nonmetallic mixing bowl with the sugar, lemon zest, and lemon juice. Split the vanilla bean in half lengthwise and scrape the seeds into the bowl, discarding the pod. Stir to combine. Set aside for 2 hours, stirring occasionally to dissolve the sugar.

Beat the cream with an electric beater until very stiff peaks form. Gently fold in the limoncello mixture, 2 tablespoons at a time. Divide the syllabub among 6 glasses and refrigerate for 5 hours. Serve accompanied by almond tuile cookies.

Limoncello, or lemoncello, is a refreshing bittersweet lemon liqueur that has been popular for centuries. Originally a regional drink from southern Italy, limoncello can be made at home without great difficulty, requiring only lemons, whole grain alcohol, sugar, and water. For devotees, however, the best is still made in its traditional homes of Capri and the Italian Amalfi coast. It is said that the local lemons there cannot be beaten for taste and aroma—and perhaps, with that special blend of sun, sea, summer, and Italian charm, they are different from lemons grown elsewhere. Limoncello is always drunk cold and makes an excellent digestif; it is also served over ice cream or fruit salads.

lime and ricotta sponge pudding .... serves 4

THIS REFRESHING DESSERT COULDN'T BE EASIER TO MAKE, AND APART FROM THE LIME AND FRESH RICOTTA
CHEESE, YOU MAY ALREADY HAVE ALL THE INGREDIENTS ON HAND. THE QUALITY OF THE RICOTTA IS IMPORTANT—
IT SHOULD BE CRUMBLY, MOIST, AND FRESH TASTING, NOT BLAND OR DULL.

unsalted butter	1/4 cup, softened
superfine sugar	1 1/2 cups
lime zest	2 teaspoons finely grated
eggs	3, at room temperature, separated
fresh ricotta cheese or a good-quality tub of ricotta	1 1/2 cups
self-rising flour	1/4 cup
lime juice	1/4 cup
confectioners' sugar	2 teaspoons

Preheat the oven to 350°F and grease a 6-cup-capacity ovenproof dish.

Using an electric beater, beat the butter and superfine sugar with half the lime zest for 30 seconds, or until combined. Add the egg yolks, one at a time, and beat until well combined. Gradually add the ricotta and flour alternately and beat until the mixture is thick and smooth. Stir in the lime juice.

Beat the egg whites until stiff peaks form and gently fold into the ricotta mixture in two batches. Pour the mixture into the prepared dish and place in a roasting pan. Pour enough hot water into the pan to come halfway up the sides of the dish. Bake for 1 hour.

Sift the confectioners' sugar over the warm dessert and sprinkle with the remaining lime zest. Serve warm.

Alternately add spoonfuls of ricotta and spoonfuls of flour.

Make sure the mixture is thick and smooth.

Don't knock out the air when folding in the egg whites.

honeycomb and mascarpone cheesecake with white chocolate sauce

.... serves 8

THIS INDULGENT VARIATION ON THE CLASSIC CHEESECAKE FEATURES CREAM, MASCARPONE CHEESE, AND CHOCOLATE HONEYCOMB TO ENSURE A REALLY CREAMY, RICH RESULT. AND TO TOP IT OFF—A DECADENT WHITE CHOCOLATE SAUCE.

graham crackers	3 1/2 ounces
unsalted butter	1/4 cup, melted
gelatin	half a 1/4-ounce envelope (or 1 1/2 teaspoons powdered)
heavy whipping cream	1 1/4 cups
eggs	2, at room temperature, separated
mascarpone cheese	1 cup
superfine sugar	1/3 cup
natural vanilla extract	1 teaspoon
chocolate-covered honeycomb bar	1 3/4 ounces, crushed (see note)

white chocolate sauce

good-quality white chocolate	heaping 3/4 cup chopped
light cream	1/3 cup

Lightly grease the base of an 8-inch springform cake pan.

Put the crackers in a food processor and process until they resemble fine crumbs. Put the melted butter in a small bowl, add the cracker crumbs, and stir to combine. Press the mixture into the base of the cake pan. Refrigerate for 15 minutes.

Put 2 tablespoons of water in a small bowl, sprinkle with the gelatin, and set aside for 2 minutes to sponge and swell. Meanwhile, heat the cream in a small saucepan until it reaches the simmering point. Remove the saucepan from heat. Add the sponged gelatin to the saucepan and stir until the gelatin has dissolved. Set aside to cool.

Beat the egg yolks, the mascarpone cheese, 1/4 cup of the sugar, and the vanilla in a small bowl with an electric beater until smooth. Fold in the crushed honeycomb bar. Add the cream mixture and mix well.

Beat the egg whites and remaining sugar until stiff peaks form. Fold into the mascarpone mixture with a metal spoon, then pour into the pan over the base and refrigerate overnight.

To make the white chocolate sauce, put the white chocolate and cream in a small heatproof bowl and place over a small saucepan of simmering water, making sure the base of the bowl doesn't touch the water. Stir until melted and smooth, then set aside to cool slightly.

To serve, cut the cheesecake into slices and drizzle with the white chocolate sauce.

Note: Chocolate-covered honeycomb bars are available from gourmet food stores.

Gently fold in the egg whites using a metal spoon.

Melt the chocolate over gentle heat so it doesn't burn.

the perfect vanilla ice cream

It is hard to match the rich creaminess of vanilla ice cream. The best flavor comes from infusing a silky egg custard with vanilla beans, while the perfect texture is achieved by churning or whisking the mixture as it freezes to break up the ice crystals. Electric ice-cream machines do the churning for you, but the time-honored handmade method gives equally good results.

Whisk 5 egg yolks and a heaping 1/2 cup superfine sugar with an electric beater for 3 minutes, or until pale and foamy. Put 1 1/4 cups each of light cream and milk in a heavy-based saucepan. Roll 2 vanilla beans in your hands for 10 seconds, split lengthwise, and add them to the saucepan. Bring the mixture to a low simmer over medium heat, then remove from heat. Whisk a little of the mixture into the egg mixture. Remove the vanilla beans and set aside. Pour the remaining cream mixture into the egg mixture, whisking constantly. Return the mixture to the clean saucepan. Cook over medium-low heat, stirring constantly with a wooden spoon, until the custard thickens enough to coat the back of a spoon. Do not allow it to boil, or it will separate. Strain into a shallow container. Scrape the seeds from the vanilla beans and stir into the custard. Set aside to cool, then refrigerate until chilled.

If using an ice-cream machine, pour in the custard and follow the manufacturer's instructions. If not, transfer the custard to the freezer. When the edges begin to freeze, whisk vigorously, then return it to the freezer until partially frozen. Whisk again, then return to the freezer. When the custard is just frozen, whisk again. Repeat once more, or until the custard is smooth, thick, and free of ice crystals. Freeze overnight. Use within 3 days. Serves 4.

  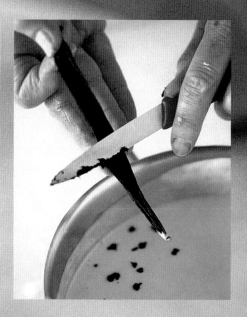

lemon pie .... serves 6–8

THIS IS PERHAPS THE CLASSIC SPRINGTIME RECIPE. SERVE IT AT ANY TIME OF THE DAY—TO COMPLETE A SPECIAL LUNCH OR DINNER, OR EVEN FOR A MORNING OR AFTERNOON SNACK. THE FILLING IS NOT DIFFICULT TO MAKE, SO YOU CAN CONCENTRATE ON PERFECTING YOUR PASTRY-MAKING TECHNIQUES.

pastry

all-purpose flour	1 1/2 cups
confectioners' sugar	1/2 cup
ground almonds	1/3 cup
unsalted butter	1/2 cup, chilled and cubed
egg yolk	1, at room temperature

filling

lemon zest	1 1/2 tablespoons finely grated
lemon juice	1/3 cup, strained
eggs	5, at room temperature
superfine sugar	3/4 cup
heavy whipping cream	1 1/4 cups
confectioners' sugar	for dusting
heavy cream	to serve

To make the pastry, put the flour, confectioners' sugar, ground almonds, and butter in a food processor and process until the mixture resembles fine crumbs. Add the egg yolk and process until the dough just comes together. Knead gently and briefly on a lightly floured surface until the dough is smooth. Form into a ball, flatten into a disk, cover with plastic wrap, and refrigerate for 30 minutes.

Preheat the oven to 350°F and grease an 8 1/2-inch loose-bottom pie pan. Roll out the pastry between two sheets of baking paper to a thickness of 1/8 inch to cover the base and side of the pie pan. Peel off the top sheet of baking paper, carefully invert the pastry into the pan, and peel off the second sheet of paper. Press the pastry gently into the base and side, ensuring the pastry is level with the top of the pan. Trim off any excess pastry. Refrigerate for 10 minutes.

Line the pastry with a sheet of crumpled baking paper and pour in some baking beads or uncooked rice. Place the pan on a baking sheet and bake for 10 minutes. Remove the paper and beads and return to the oven for another 10–15 minutes, or until lightly golden. Set aside to cool. Reduce the oven to 275°F.

To make the filling, put the lemon zest, lemon juice, eggs, sugar, and cream in a bowl and whisk until combined. Set aside for 10 minutes to allow the lemon zest to infuse the mixture, then strain the mixture. Carefully pour the filling into the pastry shell and bake for 45–50 minutes, or until just set. Set aside to cool for 10 minutes, then refrigerate until cold.

Dust the lemon pie with confectioners' sugar and serve with heavy cream.

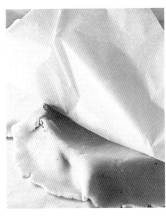
Use the baking paper to help transfer the pastry into the pan.

Lining the paper with baking beads stops the pastry from bubbling.

chocolate almondine semifreddo .... serves 6

LITERALLY MEANING "HALF COLD" IN ITALIAN, A SEMIFREDDO IS A CHILLED OR PARTLY FROZEN ICE CREAM-STYLE DESSERT. IT IS EASIER TO MAKE THAN ICE CREAM, HOWEVER, AS THERE IS NO NEED TO CHURN OR WHISK THE FROZEN MIXTURE. THE SEMIFREDDO IS BEST EATEN WITHIN 4 TO 5 DAYS.

superfine sugar	1/3 cup
almonds	1/2 cup
light cream	2 1/2 cups
eggs	2, at room temperature, separated
confectioners' sugar	1 cup
cocoa powder	heaping 1/3 cup, sifted
cream liqueur, such as Baileys	2 tablespoons
toasted flaked almonds	to serve

Lay a sheet of baking paper on a flat heatproof surface. Put the superfine sugar and 1 teaspoon of cold water in a heavy-based frying pan. Heat over medium heat until the sugar begins to melt and change color. Do not stir, but slowly turn the pan to swirl the contents together. When all the sugar has melted and turned golden, after about 6–8 minutes, remove the pan from heat, add the almonds, and swirl the pan to coat. Immediately pour the mixture onto the baking paper in a thin layer and leave to set for 20 minutes. Roughly break up the toffee with your hands, then chop it in a food processor until medium–fine.

Pour about 3/4 cup of the cream into a small saucepan and heat for 3–4 minutes, or until hot but not boiling. Whisk the egg yolks and half the confectioners' sugar in a large bowl until pale. Whisk in the cocoa powder. Add the hot cream and whisk until smooth.

Whip the remaining cream until soft peaks form. In a separate clean bowl, whisk the egg whites until soft peaks form, then gradually add the remaining confectioners' sugar and continue whisking until thick and glossy. Using a metal spoon, gently fold the cream into the chocolate custard, then fold in the egg white mixture. Sprinkle half the crushed almond toffee onto the chocolate mixture and fold through, then repeat with the remaining almond toffee. Fold in the liqueur.

Line six 1-cup metal molds with two thin strips of foil to use as handles when unmolding the semifreddo. Divide the chocolate mixture among the molds. Cover the tops with foil and freeze for at least 24 hours.

To serve, transfer the molds to the refrigerator for 5 minutes, then use the foil handles to unmold the semifreddo. Top each with flaked almonds and serve immediately.

Don't stir the caramel; swirl the pan instead.

Work quickly, as the nuts and caramel will set immediately.

lemon, fig, and walnut cake with honey yogurt

serves 8–10

THIS DELIGHTFUL CAKE FEATURES ALMOST ALL OF THE CLASSIC ELEMENTS OF MEDITERRANEAN FOOD: FIGS, WALNUTS, LEMON, WHEAT, AND OLIVE OIL. THE ONLY ELEMENT MISSING, OF COURSE, IS THE VINE, WHICH CAN BE EASILY INTRODUCED WITH A LITTLE GLASS OF SOMETHING APPROPRIATE.

superfine sugar	1/2 cup
fine semolina	2 1/2 cups
ground almonds	1 1/2 cups
baking powder	3 teaspoons
baking soda	1/2 teaspoon
lemon	1, zested and juiced
olive oil	1/2 cup
eggs	2, at room temperature, beaten
plain yogurt	3/4 cup
milk	1/2 cup
chopped walnuts	1/2 cup
fresh or semidried figs	7 chopped, plus 4 sliced figs for decoration

honey yogurt

plain yogurt	1 cup
honey	1/4 cup
natural vanilla extract	2 teaspoons

Preheat the oven to 350°F and grease and line a 9-inch square cake pan.

Combine the sugar, semolina, ground almonds, baking powder, and baking soda in a large bowl. In a separate bowl, combine the lemon zest, lemon juice, olive oil, eggs, yogurt, and milk, then stir the lemon mixture into the semolina mixture. Fold in the walnuts and chopped figs. Pour the mixture into the pan, smooth the top, and decorate with the extra sliced figs. Bake for 40 minutes, or until a skewer comes out clean when inserted into the cake.

Meanwhile, to make the honey yogurt, put the yogurt, honey, and vanilla in a small bowl and stir to combine. Keep refrigerated until needed.

Serve the warm cake accompanied by the honey yogurt.

A venerable old nut, the walnut has been cultivated since ancient Greek times. There are numerous varieties, but the most common is the nut first grown by the ancient Persians: the Persian (English) walnut. When young, green walnuts can be eaten whole (but beware of their sour taste) or pickled. The mature nut has a hard shell, and the nut within is separated into two halves by an inedible papery membrane. Walnuts are used in sweet and savory dishes, ground into flour, or pressed to release their oil. Store walnuts in their shells for up to three months in a cool, dry place, and store shelled nuts in the refrigerator for up to six months.

profiteroles with coffee mascarpone and bittersweet chocolate sauce . . . . makes 16

CHOUX PASTRY DEPENDS FOR ITS SUCCESS ON STICKING CLOSELY TO THE RECIPE, BUT IT IS NOT NECESSARILY DIFFICULT TO MAKE. CHOUX IS CRISP AND WONDERFULLY LIGHT, AND PERFECT FOR FILLING WITH INDULGENT FLAVORS. THE PROFITEROLES SHOULD BE EATEN FAIRLY SOON AFTER FILLING, OR THE PASTRY WILL GET SOGGY.

all-purpose flour	1 cup
unsalted butter	1/4 cup, cubed
salt	1/2 teaspoon
eggs	4, at room temperature

filling

instant coffee granules	2 tablespoons
boiling water	1 tablespoon
mascarpone cheese	1 cup
confectioners' sugar	2 tablespoons

chocolate sauce

good-quality	2/3 cup chopped
bittersweet chocolate	
unsalted butter	1 1/2 tablespoons
light cream	1/3 cup

Preheat the oven to 400°F and lightly grease two baking sheets.

Sift the flour onto a large piece of baking paper. Put the butter, salt, and 1 cup of water into a saucepan and bring to a boil, stirring occasionally. Using the baking paper as a funnel, pour the flour quickly into the boiling mixture. Reduce the heat to low, then beat vigorously with a wooden spoon until the mixture leaves the side of the pan and forms a smooth ball.

Transfer the mixture to a bowl and set aside to cool until it is lukewarm. Using an electric beater, beat in the eggs, one at a time, until the mixture is thick and glossy.

Using two spoons, gently drop 16 rounded balls of the mixture about 1 1/4 inches in diameter and 1 1/4 inches apart onto the prepared baking sheets. Bake for 20 minutes, or until the balls are puffed. Reduce the oven to 350°F and bake for another 10 minutes, or until the puffs are golden brown and crisp.

Using a small sharp knife, gently slit the puffs to allow the steam to escape, then return them to the oven for 10 minutes, or until the insides are dry. Set aside to cool to room temperature.

Meanwhile, to make the filling, dissolve the instant coffee in the boiling water. Set aside to cool. Beat the coffee, mascarpone, and confectioners' sugar until just combined. Be careful not to overmix, or the mascarpone mixture will separate.

To make the bittersweet chocolate sauce, put the chocolate, butter, and cream in a small heatproof bowl over a small saucepan of simmering water, making sure the base of the bowl doesn't touch the water. Stir until combined. Set aside to cool slightly.

Just before serving, slit the profiteroles in half and sandwich together with the filling. Drizzle with the bittersweet chocolate sauce, or serve the sauce separately.

vanilla custard log .... serves 6–8

IN THIS SIMPLE BUT SATISFYING DESSERT, CRISP PHYLLO ENCASES A SILKY SMOOTH CUSTARD FLAVORED WITH VANILLA AND ORANGE. DON'T BE FOOLED BY THE DELICATE APPEARANCE OF PHYLLO—IT IS SURPRISINGLY HARDY. AS YOU WORK, KEEP THE SHEETS COVERED BY A CLEAN, DAMP CLOTH; THIS WILL ENSURE THEY REMAIN PLIABLE.

milk	3 cups
cornstarch	heaping $1/3$ cup
vanilla bean	1
egg yolks	6, at room temperature
superfine sugar	$2/3$ cup
orange zest	$2^1/2$ tablespoons finely grated
phyllo pastry	8 sheets
ghee or unsalted butter	3 tablespoons, melted
confectioners' sugar	for dusting

Combine $1/4$ cup of the milk with the cornstarch and mix to a paste. Put the remaining milk in a saucepan over medium heat. Split the vanilla bean lengthwise and scrape the seeds into the pan, discarding the pod. Add the cornstarch paste, egg yolks, superfine sugar, and orange zest and whisk to combine. Boil, stirring, for 4 minutes, or until the custard is very thick. Remove from heat, cover the surface with plastic wrap, and set aside to cool.

Preheat the oven to 350°F. Line a baking sheet with baking paper.

Brush a sheet of phyllo pastry with the melted ghee or butter. Top with a second sheet of phyllo, brush with ghee or butter, then repeat with two more sheets of pastry. Repeat with the remaining pastry so you have two rectangles of pastry. Spoon half the custard along the long edge of one rectangle of pastry, leaving a $3^1/2$-inch border, and shape into a 12-inch log. Carefully lift the border side of the pastry over the custard and roll up, tucking under the sides as you roll. Repeat with the remaining custard and pastry to make a second log.

Place the rolls on the prepared sheet and brush with melted ghee or butter. Bake for 20 minutes, or until golden. Do not overcook the rolls, or the custard will leak. Set aside to cool for 10 minutes. Dust with plenty of confectioners' sugar before serving.

Stir the custard until it is very thick, then set aside to cool.

Make sure you leave a border around the custard.

Tuck in the sides as you roll up the logs.

pineapple gelato .... serves 4–6

IF USING FRESH PINEAPPLE, 3 POUNDS 5 OUNCES WILL YIELD 1 CUP OF JUICE. CHOP AND PURÉE THE FLESH IN A FOOD PROCESSOR, THEN PUSH IT THROUGH A SIEVE. FOR ADDED RETRO APPEAL, SERVE THE GELATO IN THE PINEAPPLE SHELL, WITH OR WITHOUT PAPER UMBRELLAS.

superfine sugar	1/2 cup
fresh pineapple juice	1 cup
lemon juice	1/4 cup, strained
egg white	1, at room temperature

Combine the superfine sugar with 1 cup of water in a saucepan. Stir over low heat until the sugar has dissolved. Simmer for 10 minutes, then set aside to cool completely.

Add the pineapple juice and lemon juice to the sugar syrup and mix well. Pour the mixture into a 7 x 11-inch cake pan and freeze for 1 1/2 hours, or until the mixture is just frozen.

Once the mixture is just frozen, beat the egg white until stiff peaks form. Transfer the pineapple mixture to a bowl and beat with an electric beater until smooth. Fold the beaten egg white into the pineapple mixture, then return it to the pan. Cover with plastic wrap and freeze until set.

Alternatively, put the pineapple mixture in an ice-cream machine and churn following the manufacturer's instructions until just set. Fold in the beaten egg white, pour into the cake pan, and freeze.

A native of tropical South America, the pineapple is actually several individual fruits joined together: each of these fruits are the result of numerous unfertilized flowers that have fused. To most of us, however, it is a deliciously juicy and sweet fruit, the very emblem of warm weather. Like most fruit, pineapple is best eaten fresh, but it is also used in dishes such as ice creams, sorbets, cakes, and as a sometimes controversial topping for pizza. Pineapples do not continue to ripen after being picked, so it pays to choose well. Select pineapples that are heavy for their size and sweetly aromatic.

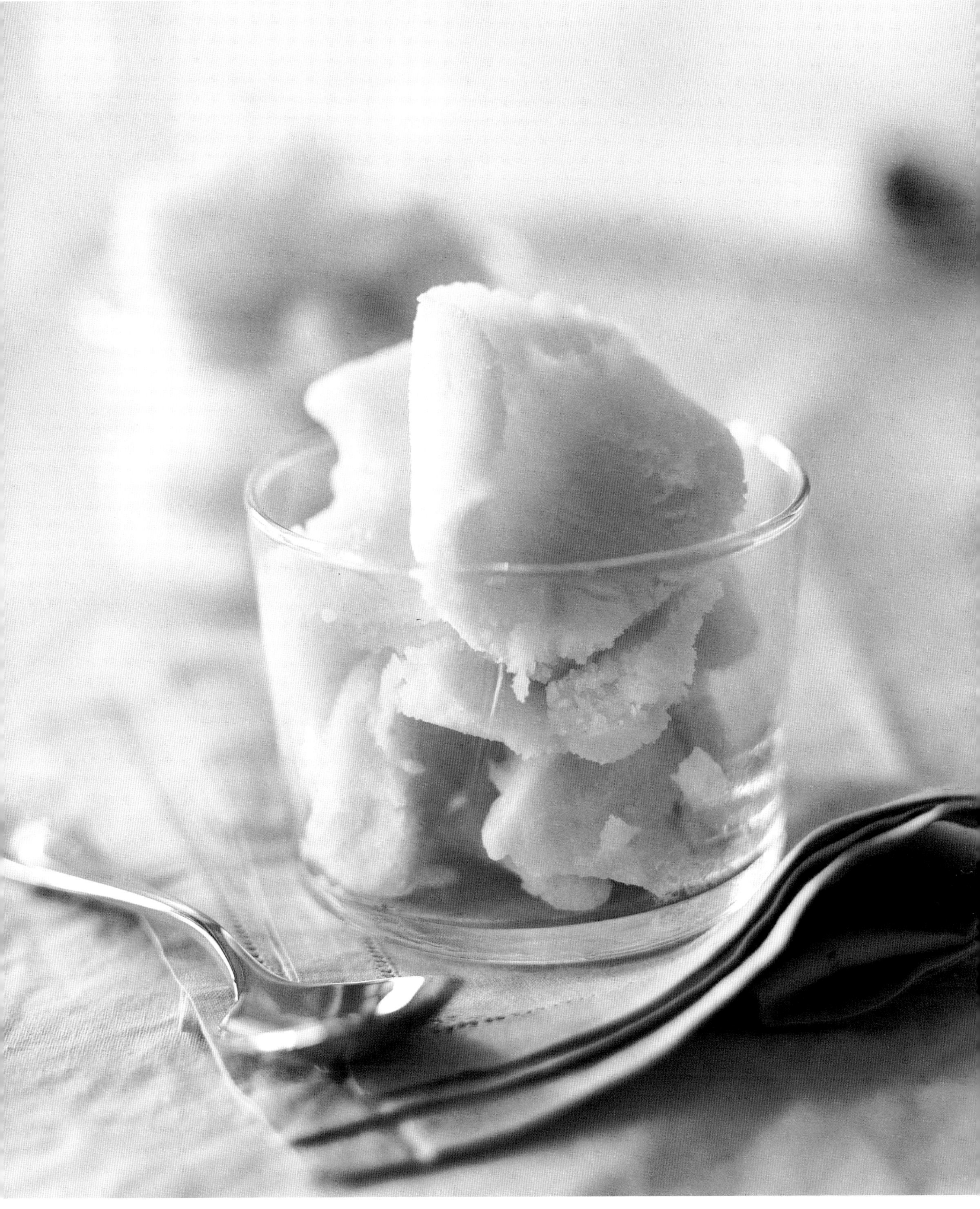

hazelnut crackle log .... serves 6–8

EARLY FORMS OF MERINGUE WERE CALLED "SUGAR PUFF," AND IT IS NOT HARD TO SEE WHY. CRISP AND CRACKLY, THE APPEAL OF MERINGUE COMES AS MUCH FROM ITS TEXTURE AS ITS TASTE. THIS MERINGUE ISN'T AS SWEET AS SOME, DUE TO THE HAZELNUTS, WHICH COMBINE WONDERFULLY WITH THE COFFEE-MASCARPONE FILLING.

meringue

roasted skinned hazelnuts	½ cup
egg whites	4, at room temperature
superfine sugar	⅔ cup
cornstarch	1 teaspoon
natural vanilla extract	1 teaspoon
white wine vinegar	1 teaspoon

filling

instant coffee	2 teaspoons
hot water	2 teaspoons
mascarpone cheese	1 cup
confectioners' sugar	2 tablespoons, sifted

To make the meringue, preheat the oven to 300°F. Draw an 8 x 14-inch rectangle on a sheet of baking paper. Put the sheet, pencil side down, on a baking sheet.

Put the hazelnuts in a food processor and process until the nuts are coarsely ground.

Whisk the egg whites in a large bowl until soft peaks form. Gradually add the sugar, 1 tablespoon at a time, and whisk until stiff and glossy. Gently fold in the hazelnuts, then the cornstarch, vanilla, and vinegar. Spoon onto the baking sheet and spread evenly inside the marked rectangle. Bake for 25 minutes, or until the meringue is set and lightly golden.

Lay a large sheet of baking paper on a work surface and invert the cooked meringue on top. Peel off the baking paper and set aside to cool for 15 minutes.

To make the filling, dissolve the instant coffee in the hot water. Put the coffee, mascarpone, and confectioners' sugar in a bowl and mix well.

Spread the filling evenly over the meringue. Starting at one short end, and using the baking paper as a lever, gently roll up the meringue. The outer surface will crack into a pattern. Serve immediately, cut into slices.

Fold the hazelnuts into the egg-white mixture.

Spread the mixture evenly using a palette knife.

Spread the filling to cover the whole meringue.

summer

This is the season when nature is at its most abundant, when exotic fruits such as delicately perfumed lychees, tart-yet-sweet passion fruits, and red papayas become wonderfully, if fleetingly, available. Berries of all colors, shapes, and sizes abound, as do stone fruits, from soft, furry peaches and apricots to firmer nectarines and cherries. Strong flavors, vibrant colors, and heady aromas proclaim the arrival of summer.

Not surprisingly, there is a fair dose of the tropical in this chapter, with desserts such as the mango ice-cream log and coconut pavlovas topped with tropical fruits and passion-fruit cream doing their best to suggest languid days by the pool. Even dishes hailing from countries not renowned for their long, hot summer days get in on the act—the traditional English dessert Eton mess goes tropical with the addition of red papaya and passion fruit. The wonderful thing about cooking with fruit is its versatility: it can make the familiar special, for example by using caramelized peaches and passion fruit in a crumble; it can provide color and at least the suggestion of healthiness to an otherwise frighteningly decadent recipe, such as the white chocolate roulade filled with vanilla cream and fresh berries; and it can also form wonderful desserts in its own right, like poached vanilla peaches with raspberry puree and passion-fruit sauce.

However, it is perhaps in the realm of ice cream and sorbet that fruit comes into its own. This chapter includes a number of superb recipes featuring peaches, mangoes, lychees, and strawberries combined with aromatic spices such as vanilla and star anise and fragrant waters such as rose water. The results look wonderful and taste divine. An ice-cream machine is handy for these desserts but not essential, and sorbet can be made with just a food processor.

Finally, though summer generally isn't the time when you want to be laboring in the kitchen, a few involved recipes have been included because they were too good to leave out—not everything needs to take only 10 minutes! Individual cheesecakes with macerated strawberries are irresistibly good—the sweet, soft fruit contrasting perfectly with the rich, smooth cheesecake. Also, instructions are given for making perfect crepes—make a batch of these, fill them with fresh fruit and your own homemade ice cream, and you are well on your way to a sensational summer.

individual cheesecakes with macerated strawberries . . . . makes 12

SERVE THESE LITTLE CHEESECAKES AT THE END OF A MEAL AND YOU WILL MAKE YOURSELF VERY POPULAR. RICH AND VELVETY, THEY ARE NOT BAKED BUT REFRIGERATED OVERNIGHT. THE ADVANTAGE OF THAT, OF COURSE, IS THAT ALL THE HARD WORK IS DONE WELL IN ADVANCE OF THE BIG OCCASION.

sweet cookie crumbs	heaping 3/4 cup
toasted flaked almonds	1 cup, lightly crushed
white chocolate	scant 2/3 cup chopped, melted
unsalted butter	1/4 cup, melted

filling

powdered gelatin	2 teaspoons
cream cheese	1 cup, softened
superfine sugar	heaping 1/3 cup
orange zest	1 teaspoon finely grated
orange juice	2 tablespoons
light cream	1/2 cup
egg white	1, at room temperature

macerated strawberries

strawberries	3 1/3 cups
superfine sugar	1 tablespoon
orange zest	1/4 teaspoon finely grated
orange juice	2 tablespoons

Lightly grease a twelve-hole standard muffin pan. Line each hole with two long strips of baking paper in the shape of a cross to help remove the cheesecakes.

Put the cookie crumbs, almonds, white chocolate, and butter in a bowl and stir until just combined, adding more butter if the mixture is too dry. Divide the mixture among the muffin holes and use your fingers to press it over the bases and up the sides, smoothing with the back of a spoon. Refrigerate the crusts while preparing the filling.

To make the filling, put 1 tablespoon of water in a small bowl and sprinkle with the gelatin. Leave the gelatin to sponge and swell.

Beat the cream cheese, sugar, and orange zest in a small bowl with an electric beater until light and creamy. Beat in the orange juice until combined. Stir in the gelatin mixture.

Whip the cream until soft peaks form. In a separate bowl, whisk the egg white with a clean whisk until soft peaks form. Fold the cream and egg white into the cream-cheese mixture. Spoon into the prepared crusts and refrigerate for several hours, overnight, or until set.

To make the macerated strawberries, cut the strawberries into small pieces. Combine the strawberries with the sugar, orange zest, and orange juice and refrigerate for several hours.

To serve, carefully remove the cheesecakes from the muffin pan and top with a spoonful of strawberries.

Smooth the cookie crust with the back of a spoon.

Leave the strawberries for several hours to soak up the sauce.

tropical eton mess

THIS DESSERT MAKES NO PRETENSE OF SOPHISTICATION, WHICH MEANS IT WILL BE A SUREFIRE WINNER WITH EVERYONE. THE FRUIT CAN BE CHANGED TO MATCH THE SEASON, THOUGH STICK WITH FRUITS THAT ARE JUICY BUT FIRM—YOU DON'T WANT A MUSHY MESS. IF YOU CHANGE THE FRUIT, SELECT COMPLEMENTARY LIQUEURS.

meringue

egg white	1, at room temperature
superfine sugar	1/4 cup
cornstarch	1/4 teaspoon
passion fruits	4
strawberries	heaping 3/4 cup, thickly sliced
small red papaya	1/2, seeded, peeled, and cubed
superfine sugar	1 tablespoon
raspberry liqueur, such as Framboise, or orange liqueur, such as Grand Marnier	1 tablespoon, optional
heavy whipping cream	2/3 cup
plain yogurt	scant 3/4 cup

To make the meringue, preheat the oven to 250°F and line a cookie sheet with baking paper.

Beat the egg white until stiff peaks form. Add 1 tablespoon of the superfine sugar and beat for 3 minutes, or until glossy. Add another tablespoon of sugar and beat for another 3 minutes. Add the remaining sugar and the cornstarch and beat for 2 minutes.

Put four even-sized heaping spoonfuls of the meringue mixture on the prepared sheet. Bake the meringues for 30 minutes, or until they are firm on the outside. Turn off the oven and leave the meringues in the oven until the oven is cold. Roughly crumble the meringues.

Cut the passion fruits in half and scoop out the flesh and edible seeds. Combine the strawberries, papaya, and half the passion-fruit pulp (flesh and seeds) in a bowl. Stir in the sugar and the liqueur, if using. Set aside for 5 minutes, or until ready to assemble.

Just before serving, beat the cream in a bowl until thick. Stir in the yogurt. Add the fruit mixture all at once and stir until roughly combined. Spoon half the mixture into tall, 1 1/4-cup parfait glasses. Top with the crumbled meringue and then the remaining fruit. Garnish with the remaining passion-fruit pulp and serve immediately.

Use two spoons to help put the meringue mixture on the sheet.

Combine the fruit with the sugar and liqueur.

Mix the cream, yogurt, and fruit together briefly.

cherry clafouti

FEW FRUITS ARRIVE WITH THE SORT OF UNBRIDLED COLOR AND ABUNDANCE SHOWN BY CHERRIES EACH SUMMER. UNDOUBTEDLY, SUMMER IS THE BEST TIME TO MAKE THIS RECIPE. OUT OF SEASON, YOU CAN USE 3½ CUPS OF WELL-DRAINED, CANNED, PITTED CHERRIES; MORELLO SOUR CHERRIES WILL GIVE THE BEST RESULT.

cherries	2½ cups pitted, stems removed
all-purpose flour	½ cup
superfine sugar	heaping ⅓ cup
salt	pinch
eggs	2, at room temperature, lightly beaten
milk	heaping ¾ cup
natural vanilla extract	1 teaspoon
unsalted butter	1½ tablespoons, melted
confectioners' sugar	for dusting

Preheat the oven to 415°F and lightly grease a 6-cup-capacity round ovenproof dish.

Spread the cherries evenly over the base of the prepared dish.

Put the flour, superfine sugar, and pinch of salt in a bowl and stir to combine. Add the eggs and beat until well combined. Combine the milk, vanilla, and butter, then pour into the egg mixture and beat until combined.

Carefully pour the batter over the cherries and bake for 40 minutes, or until the cherry clafouti is golden brown. Set aside to cool for at least 10 minutes, then serve warm or cold, dusted with confectioners' sugar.

The glossy, deep-red cherry has been celebrated throughout the centuries by artists, poets, gardeners, and cooks alike. A relative of the plum, peach, and apricot, cherries are available in many varieties, which are classified as either sweet, sour, or hybrid. Sweet cherries and hybrids can be eaten raw or cooked, while sour cherries are mostly reserved for cooking—for example, in pies and jams. When buying cherries, look at the stems: they should be soft and pliable, not brown and brittle. Sweet cherries can be stored in the refrigerator for up to one week, and sour cherries for several weeks. Cherries are also used to make Kirsch and maraschino liqueur.

blueberry crumble cake .... serves 8–10

THIS CAKE IS QUICK AND EASY TO MAKE AND, APART FROM A FEW FRESH INGREDIENTS, RELIES ON STORE-SHELF STAPLES. IT HAS A SATISFYING, FIRM TEXTURE AND CRUMBLY, SWEET TOPPING. BLUEBERRIES ARE MOST OFTEN PAIRED WITH ALMONDS, BUT HERE PECANS ARE USED FOR AN EQUALLY GOOD EFFECT.

all-purpose flour	1 cup
whole-wheat all-purpose flour	3/4 cup
superfine sugar	1 cup
baking powder	2 1/2 teaspoons
ground cinnamon	1/2 teaspoon
blueberries	1 cup
egg	1, at room temperature
milk	3/4 cup
oil	1/3 cup
natural vanilla extract	1 teaspoon
lemon	1, zest finely grated
heavy cream	to serve

topping

pecans	1/2 cup chopped
soft brown sugar	1/3 cup
all-purpose flour	1/4 cup
blueberries	1 cup
oil	2 tablespoons

Preheat the oven to 375°F and grease an 8-inch springform cake pan.

Sift the flours, sugar, baking powder, and cinnamon into a large bowl. Return the husks collected in the sieve to the bowl. Toss the blueberries through the flour mixture.

Whisk together the egg, milk, oil, vanilla, and lemon zest. Pour into the dry ingredients and stir to combine. Pour the mixture into the prepared pan.

To make the topping, combine the pecans, brown sugar, flour, and blueberries in a bowl and sprinkle evenly over the cake. Drizzle the oil over the topping.

Bake the cake for 50–55 minutes, or until a skewer comes out clean when inserted into the cake. Serve the cake warm with a dollop of heavy cream.

Toss the blueberries through the dry ingredients.

Combine the egg mixture with the dry ingredients.

Sprinkle the topping evenly over the cake.

mango ice-cream log .... serves 8–10

UNLIKE MANY ICE CREAMS, WHICH ARE SERVED AS AN ACCOMPANIMENT, THIS ICE-CREAM LOG DESERVES TO TAKE CENTER STAGE. THE GOLDEN FRUITY FRESHNESS OF THE MANGO PROVIDES A CONTRAST TO THE CREAMY LAYERS SURROUNDING IT. SERVE THE ICE CREAM WITH ALMOND BISCOTTI OR OTHER THIN, CRISP COOKIES.

light cream	2 cups
milk	1 cup
vanilla bean	1, split lengthwise
egg yolks	6, at room temperature
superfine sugar	½ cup
mangoes	2 large, flesh pureed

Put the cream and milk in a saucepan. Scrape the seeds from the vanilla bean into the saucepan and add the vanilla pod. Heat over medium heat until the mixture is hot but not boiling. Remove from heat and discard the vanilla pod.

Using an electric beater, beat the egg yolks and superfine sugar in a large bowl until thick and pale. Slowly pour the hot cream mixture onto the egg mixture, whisking continuously. Pour the custard into a clean saucepan and stir over low heat for 5–6 minutes, or until the custard is thick enough to coat the back of a spoon. Refrigerate until completely cold.

Pour the custard into an ice-cream machine and churn according to the manufacturer's instructions. Alternatively, pour the custard into a metal bowl and freeze for 2–2½ hours, or until set around the edges but still soft in the middle; beat with an electric beater for 3 minutes, or until the custard is smooth again. Once the mixture is churned or smooth, pour half the mixture into a 8 x 4-inch loaf pan lined with plastic wrap. Refrigerate the remaining mixture until required. Carefully spoon the mango puree over the mixture in the pan and freeze for 1 hour. Top with the remaining ice cream mixture and freeze overnight.

To serve, dip the base of the pan in hot water for 5 seconds, then invert the ice cream onto a serving plate and cut into slices.

The easiest way to access the flesh is to cut into the cheeks.

Carefully spoon the mango puree over the first layer of ice cream.

Add the top layer of ice cream after freezing the log for 1 hour.

poached vanilla peaches with raspberry puree and passion-fruit sauce .... serves 4

THIS DELIGHTFUL DESSERT IS EXACTLY WHAT SUMMER ENTERTAINING SHOULD BE ALL ABOUT: A SIMPLE, QUICK RECIPE, FULL OF FLAVOR AND COLOR, THAT UTILIZES THE BEST OF THE SEASON'S PRODUCE. YOU WILL NEED ABOUT THREE PASSION FRUITS FOR THIS RECIPE.

superfine sugar	1 1/2 cups
vanilla bean	1, halved lengthwise
peaches	4
fresh raspberries or frozen raspberries, thawed	heaping 3/4 cup
vanilla ice cream	4 small scoops

passion-fruit sauce

passion-fruit pulp	1/4 cup
superfine sugar	2 tablespoons

Put the sugar, vanilla bean, and 2 1/2 cups of water in a large saucepan. Stir over low heat until the sugar has dissolved. Bring to a slow boil, then add the peaches and simmer for 5 minutes, or until the peaches are just tender and softened. Cool the peaches in the syrup, then remove with a slotted spoon. Peel and halve the peaches, removing the stones.

Put the raspberries in a food processor and process until pureed. Push the raspberries through a sieve, discarding the pulp.

To make the passion-fruit sauce, combine the passion-fruit pulp with the sugar and stir until the sugar has dissolved.

To serve, divide the raspberry puree among four glasses. Arrange a scoop of ice cream and two peach halves on top. Spoon over the passion-fruit sauce and serve immediately.

This fragrant, juicy stone fruit is instantly recognizable by its rosy-pink, downy skin. Inside, the flesh of the peach may be yellow or white, separating easily from the stone (freestone) or not (clingstone). Peaches do not last long, so buy only as many as can be eaten or cooked within the space of three to four days. Avoid bruised or soft peaches; the latter will taste floury and will be sadly disappointing. Apart from enjoying their succulent flesh just as it is, peaches are excellent for poaching in wine or syrup and for using in pies, sorbets, and sauces.

apricot meringue torte . . . . serves 8–10

APRICOTS COMBINE WELL WITH BOTH SAVORY AND SWEET FLAVORS, BUT THEIR SHORT SEASON MEANS THEY DON'T OFTEN MAKE IT INTO THE KITCHEN—A GREAT PITY, AS THIS DESSERT SHOWS. IF USING FRESH APRICOTS, MAKE SURE THEY ARE SWEET, FIRM, AND RIPE; OTHERWISE USE CANNED APRICOTS.

superfine sugar	1²/3 cups
cinnamon stick	1
natural vanilla extract	2 teaspoons
apricots	1 pound, quartered, stones removed
egg whites	6, at room temperature
white vinegar	1¹/2 teaspoons
ground hazelnuts	¹/3 cup
heavy whipping cream	1¹/4 cups
confectioners' sugar	for dusting

Combine 1¹/2 cups of water, a heaping ¹/2 cup of the sugar, the cinnamon stick, and 1 teaspoon of the vanilla in a large saucepan. Stir over low heat until the sugar has dissolved. Increase the heat to medium and simmer for 15 minutes. Add the quartered apricots and simmer over low heat for another 40 minutes, or until the apricots are thick and pulpy. Set aside to cool.

Preheat the oven to 300°F and draw an 8¹/2-inch circle on two sheets of baking paper. Put the sheets, pencil side down, on two cookie sheets.

Beat the egg whites in a bowl until stiff peaks form. Add the remaining sugar, a little at a time, and continue beating until the mixture is stiff and glossy. Beat in the vinegar and remaining vanilla. Gently fold in the ground hazelnuts.

Divide the meringue mixture between the two circles on the prepared sheets and smooth the surface. Bake for 35–40 minutes, or until the meringues are firm and dry. Turn off the oven and leave the meringues in the oven to cool completely.

Peel off the baking paper and place one meringue disk on a serving plate. Whip the cream until stiff peaks form. Discard the cinnamon stick from the syrup and drain the apricots. Gently stir the apricots through the whipped cream and spread over the meringue. Place the second meringue disk on top of the apricot cream and dust with confectioners' sugar.

Simmer the apricots until thick and pulpy.

Gently stir the apricot mixture into the cream.

mango and star-anise sorbet with honey macadamia wafers

USE THE HONEY MACADAMIA WAFERS AS SPOONS FOR SCOOPING UP THIS SUMMER SORBET: SMOOTH, GENTLY PERFUMED SORBET AGAINST SWEET, NUTTY CRUNCHINESS. PERFECT. STAR ANISE WILL BRING A SUBTLE ANISEED FLAVOR TO THE SORBET.

superfine sugar	heaping 3/4 cup
star anise	2
lemon juice	1 tablespoon
mangoes	3, flesh chopped to give 1 pound 2 ounces
egg white	1, at room temperature

honey macadamia wafers

egg white	1, at room temperature
superfine sugar	1/4 cup
honey	2 tablespoons
all-purpose flour	2 tablespoons, sifted
unsalted butter	3 tablespoons, melted and cooled
macadamia nuts	3/4 cup chopped

Combine the sugar with 1 1/4 cups water and the star anise in a saucepan. Stir over medium heat until the sugar has dissolved. Bring to a boil, then reduce the heat and simmer for 1 minute. Set aside to cool to room temperature. Stir in the lemon juice.

Put the mango in a food processor and puree until smooth. Strain the sugar syrup onto the mango and process until just combined, then transfer to a shallow metal container, cover, and freeze. When the sorbet is three-quarters frozen, transfer it to a food processor, add the egg white, and blend until smooth. Return the sorbet to the container and freeze until required.

To make the honey macadamia wafers, preheat the oven to 400°F. Line two 12-inch square baking sheets with baking paper. Put the egg white in a small bowl and beat with an electric beater until soft peaks form. Gradually add the sugar and continue beating until the sugar has dissolved. Beat in the honey and then fold in the flour and butter. Spread the mixture very thinly over the prepared sheets, then sprinkle evenly with the macadamia nuts. Bake for 7–10 minutes, or until lightly golden. Set aside to cool on the sheets, then break into pieces. Store in an airtight container, because the wafers will soften if left out. Serve scoops of mango sorbet accompanied by large pieces of the honey macadamia wafers.

Strain the star-anise syrup onto the mango puree.

Sprinkle the macadamia nuts in an even layer.

three ways with raspberries

BURSTING WITH COLOR AND FLAVOR, RASPBERRIES ARE NOT REALLY TEAM PLAYERS—NOT WHERE OTHER FRUITS ARE CONCERNED ANYWAY. INSTEAD, THEY PREFER THE COMPANY OF INGREDIENTS SUCH AS CREAM, CHOCOLATE, AND CHAMPAGNE. FRESH RASPBERRIES ARE DELICATE AND SHOULD BE HANDLED AS LITTLE AS POSSIBLE. THEY DO FREEZE WELL, HOWEVER, SO IF YOU ARE IN NEED OF A LITTLE CHEER DURING WINTER, MAKE THE RICE PUDDING WITH FROZEN RASPBERRIES: A BOLD DASH OF RASPBERRY CUTTING THROUGH WHITE CHOCOLATE CREAMINESS.

raspberry and orange trifle

Combine 2 cups good-quality store-bought custard, 1 heaping cup mascarpone cheese, $1/2$ cup pureed raspberries, $1/3$ cup confectioners' sugar, and $1 1/4$ cups lightly crushed store-bought meringues. Arrange 9 ounces sliced plain orange cake or 4 sliced orange muffins in the base of a large glass dish or six dessert glasses. Sprinkle $1/4$ cup orange liqueur, such as Cointreau, over the cake, then sprinkle with 2 cups raspberries. Spoon the custard mixture over the raspberries and top with another 1 cup raspberries and $1 1/4$ cups crushed meringues. Chill until ready to serve. Dust with sifted confectioners' sugar, if desired. Serves 6.

raspberry, lemongrass, and sparkling rosé jellies

Put $3 1/4$ cups raspberries, 1 cup superfine sugar, 2 bruised lemongrass stems, $1/4$ cup lemon juice, and $1 1/2$ cups sparkling rosé in a saucepan. Slowly bring to a boil. Boil for 1 minute, then set aside for 30 minutes. Strain the mixture through cheesecloth into a bowl, discarding the pulp. Return the liquid to a clean saucepan and heat to just below the boiling point. Whisk in $4 1/2$ teaspoons powdered gelatin until dissolved. Set aside to cool. Stir another $1 1/2$ cups sparkling rosé into the raspberry liquid. Divide a heaping $3/4$ cup raspberries among six champagne flutes. Pour a little of the raspberry syrup into each glass to set the raspberries, then refrigerate. Refrigerate the remaining jelly until it is cold and near the setting point. Whisk the cold jelly to create bubbles, then pour it into the glasses and chill until set. Serves 6.

white chocolate and raspberry ripple rice pudding

Using a hand blender, puree 1 cup fresh raspberries, 2 tablespoons confectioners' sugar, and 2 tablespoons raspberry liqueur, such as Framboise. Melt 2 tablespoons unsalted butter in a large nonstick saucepan. Add a heaping $1/2$ cup risotto and 1 split vanilla bean and stir until the rice is coated in the butter. Heat 3 cups milk, $1/4$ cup superfine sugar, and 1 teaspoon natural vanilla extract to just below the boiling point. Ladle a spoonful of the milk mixture into the rice and stir constantly until the liquid has been absorbed. Repeat the process until all the milk mixture has been added. Remove the vanilla bean. Add $2/3$ cup chopped white chocolate and stir until the chocolate has melted. Set aside for 5 minutes, then spoon the rice pudding into bowls. Swirl the raspberry puree through the rice to create a ripple effect. Serves 4.

lychee and strawberry ice cream................serves 6–8

ANYONE WHO HAS NEVER TRIED LYCHEES BEFORE WILL WONDER WHAT GIVES THIS ICE CREAM SUCH A WONDERFUL PERFUMED SWEETNESS——SOMETHING BESIDES THE STRAWBERRIES. THESE TWO FRUITS COMBINE VERY WELL, DESPITE THE FACT THAT ONE IS FROM TEMPERATE REGIONS AND THE OTHER NATIVE TO TROPICAL CHINA.

strawberries	1²/3 cups
superfine sugar	³/4 cup
lychees in syrup	20-ounce can
milk	1¹/2 cups
light cream	2 cups
egg yolks	6, at room temperature

Reserve ¹/3 cup of the strawberries for decoration. Hull and roughly chop the remaining strawberries and place in a bowl, along with any juices. Sprinkle with 1 tablespoon of the sugar and set aside for 30 minutes. Drain and finely chop the lychees, reserving ¹/2 cup of the syrup.

Put the milk, cream, and remaining sugar in a saucepan over medium heat. Cook, stirring constantly, for a few minutes, or until the sugar has dissolved and the milk is just about to boil. Remove from heat.

Whisk the egg yolks in a bowl for 1 minute, or until combined, then add ¹/4 cup of the hot milk mixture. Stir to combine, then pour into the remaining milk mixture. Return the saucepan to low–medium heat and cook, stirring constantly with a wooden spoon, until the mixture thickens and coats the back of the spoon. Do not allow the mixture to boil. Strain through a fine sieve and set aside to cool.

Gently stir the strawberries and any juice, lychees, and lychee syrup into the custard to combine. Transfer to an ice-cream machine and freeze according to the manufacturer's instructions. Alternatively, transfer to a shallow metal tray and freeze, whisking every couple of hours until the ice cream is frozen and creamy in texture. Serve the ice cream with the reserved strawberries.

Leave the chopped strawberries to soak up the sugar.

Strain the custard to give a silky-smooth ice cream.

nectarine feuilletées . . . . makes 8

WHEN NECTARINES ARE IN FULL FLIGHT IN SUMMER, IT'S NICE TO BE ABLE TO GRAB A HANDFUL AND MAKE A FABULOUS DESSERT WITHOUT HAVING TO THINK ABOUT IT TOO MUCH. THIS IS JUST SUCH A DESSERT. THE NAME OF THIS RECIPE COMES FROM THE FRENCH *PÂTÉ FEUILLETÉE*, MEANING "PUFF PASTRY."

frozen butter puff pastry	2 sheets, thawed
unsalted butter	1/4 cup, softened
ground almonds	1/2 cup
natural vanilla extract	1/2 teaspoon
nectarines	5 large
superfine sugar	1/4 cup
apricot or peach jam	1/3 cup, warmed and sieved

Preheat the oven to 400°F. Line two large baking sheets with baking paper.

Cut the pastry sheets into eight 4 1/2-inch rounds and place on the prepared sheets. Combine the butter, ground almonds, and vanilla in a small bowl to form a paste. Divide the paste among the pastry rounds and spread evenly, leaving a 3/4-inch border around the edge.

Halve the nectarines, removing the stones, and cut them into 1/4-inch slices. Arrange the nectarine slices over the pastry rounds, overlapping the slices and leaving a thin border. Sprinkle the sugar over the nectarines.

Bake for 15 minutes, or until the pastries are puffed and golden. Brush the nectarines and pastry with the warm jam while the pastries are hot. Serve hot or at room temperature.

Smooth-skinned nectarines are sometimes passed over for their downy relative, the peach, but one is not better than the other: they are just different. Peaches are sweeter and more fragrant; nectarines are richer—their name stems from the Greek word for nectar. Like peaches, however, their flesh may be white or yellow, freestone or clingstone, with the white-fleshed fruit generally considered the most flavorsome. Nectarines are best bought fresh, not canned. Select fruits that have good color and smell, ripe but not to the point of being soft and squishy. Nectarines can be poached, stuffed and baked, broiled, and added to pies and pastries.

aromatic peaches with
sweetened yogurt . . . . serves 4

THIS FRAGRANT, HEADY DESSERT INFUSES PEACHES WITH FOUR DIFFERENT SPICES——A DELECTABLE DISH TAKING
FULL ADVANTAGE OF THE SEASON'S STONE FRUITS. MACERATE THE PEACHES IN THE SYRUP FOR NO LONGER THAN
4 HOURS, OR THE PEACHES WILL DISCOLOR AND LOSE THEIR BEAUTIFUL BLUSH.

superfine sugar	1 cup
vanilla bean	1, split lengthwise
cinnamon stick	1
cardamom pods	6
star anise	2
peaches	4
dark brown sugar	2 tablespoons
plain yogurt	1¼ cups

Pour 2 cups of water into a saucepan and add the superfine sugar. Heat over medium heat until the sugar has dissolved. Scrape the seeds from the vanilla bean into the saucepan and add the pod, cinnamon stick, cardamom pods, and star anise. Boil for 2 minutes, then set aside to cool.

Put the peaches in a heatproof bowl and cover with boiling water. Set aside for 1 minute, then drain the peaches and refresh in ice-cold water. Halve the peaches, removing the stones and skin. Working quickly to prevent the peaches from browning, place the peaches in a bowl and strain the cooled syrup over them. Refrigerate for several hours to allow the peaches to macerate in the syrup.

Stir the dark brown sugar through the yogurt and serve with the peaches and syrup.

Infuse the syrup with the aromatic spices.

Soak the peaches in boiling water to make them easy to peel.

Sweeten the yogurt with a little dark brown sugar.

strawberry and
mascarpone mousse .... serves 6

FOR A TRIPLE-CREAM CHEESE, MASCARPONE IS NOT OVERLY SWEET. IT IS, HOWEVER, VERY RICH, MELLOW, AND WONDERFULLY SMOOTH. IT PROVIDES THE PERFECT BASE FOR THE STRAWBERRIES AND CRUNCHY PRALINE. THIS RECIPE IS A GREAT ONE TO HAVE ON HAND FOR SUMMER, WHEN SWEET, JUICY STRAWBERRIES ARE AT THEIR PEAK.

superfine sugar	1/3 cup
powdered gelatin	1 tablespoon
strawberries	3 1/3 cups, hulled
mascarpone cheese	1 cup
homemade crushed praline	to serve, optional (page 27)

Combine the sugar and 1/2 cup of water in a small saucepan. Stir over low heat for 3 minutes, or until the sugar has dissolved. Sprinkle the gelatin over the sugar mixture and stir for 2 minutes, or until the gelatin has dissolved. Set aside to cool.

Put the hulled strawberries in a food processor and process until smooth. Add the mascarpone and process until well combined. With the motor running, add the gelatin mixture in a slow stream. Pour the mixture into a 4-cup mold. Refrigerate overnight, or until set.

To serve, dip the base of the mold in hot water for 10 seconds, then invert the mousse onto a plate. Top with the crushed praline, if using.

This luscious fruit needs little introduction. Native to both Europe and America, the strawberry is grown in temperate regions around the world and is often available year-round. Look out for wild species, too, which can be more flavorsome than the cultivated varieties. The strawberry is unique in that the seeds grow around the outside of the fruit rather than inside it. Versatile and robust, strawberries can be used in everything from smoothies and purees to cakes and preserves. When buying, don't necessarily choose the biggest and brightest; rather, select those that are plump, glossy, unbruised, and firm. Store in the refrigerator and only wash just before eating.

coconut pavlovas with tropical fruits and passion-fruit cream .... serves 4

WHO DOESN'T GET EXCITED BY A CRISP MERINGUE BASE, LADEN WITH CREAM AND FRESH FRUIT? THE PASSION-FRUIT CREAM USED HERE IS A CLASSIC TOPPING, THOUGH THE LYCHEES AND PAPAYA ARE A SIGN OF HOW THINGS CHANGE. HOWEVER, ANY SEASONAL FRESH FRUIT CAN BE USED.

pavlovas

egg whites	2, at room temperature
superfine sugar	1/2 cup
cornstarch	1/2 teaspoon
natural vanilla extract	1/2 teaspoon
shredded dried coconut	1/4 cup

passion-fruit cream

light cream	1 cup
confectioners' sugar	2 tablespoons
passion fruits	4
red papaya	1/2 small, seeded and peeled
fresh lychees	4, halved and seeded
mango	1/2, peeled and seeded

To make the pavlovas, preheat the oven to 225°F. Line a baking sheet with baking paper.

Beat the egg whites and sugar in a bowl for 8 minutes, or until the meringue is glossy and very thick. Beat in the cornstarch and vanilla, then gently fold the shredded dried coconut through the meringue mixture with a metal spoon.

Using two large metal tablespoons, spoon four large oval-shaped spoonfuls of the meringue mixture onto the prepared sheet. Bake for 30 minutes, or until the pavlovas are crisp on the outside. Turn off the oven and leave the pavlovas in the oven until the oven is cold.

To make the passion-fruit cream, beat the cream and confectioners' sugar until firm peaks form. Fold the passion-fruit pulp through the cream and refrigerate until ready to serve.

Cut the papaya, lychees, and mango into very small diced pieces. To serve, top the pavlovas with some of the passion-fruit cream and accompany with the diced fruit.

Note: For a quick alternative, make the meringues and top with whipped cream, a selection of fresh berries, and a quick coulis made from pureed and sieved berries.

Use a metal spoon to fold in the shredded dried coconut.

Make sure the meringues are well spaced on the sheet.

Gently fold the passion-fruit pulp into the cream.

white chocolate and berry roulade

.... serves 6–8

IT IS REMARKABLE HOW MANY SUPERB CREATIONS CAN BE MADE OUT OF THE BASIC ELEMENTS OF FLOUR, EGGS,
SUGAR, AND CREAM. ROULADES CAN BE SAVORY, THOUGH THIS ONE MOST CERTAINLY ISN'T. BUY THE BEST JUICY
BERRIES YOU CAN FIND TO REALLY BRING IT ALIVE.

eggs	4, at room temperature, separated
superfine sugar	1/2 cup, plus 1–2 tablespoons, plus extra, for sprinkling
hot water	1 tablespoon
white chocolate	heaping 1/3 cup finely grated
self-rising flour	1/2 cup
strawberries	2/3 cup sliced
fresh raspberries	heaping 3/4 cup
heavy whipping cream	3/4 cup
confectioners' sugar	2 teaspoons, plus extra, for dusting
natural vanilla extract	1 teaspoon

Preheat the oven to 400°F. Lightly grease a 10 x 12-inch jelly-roll pan with oil. Line the pan with baking paper, allowing the paper to hang over the two long sides.

Beat the egg yolks and sugar with an electric beater for 5 minutes, or until very thick and creamy. Fold in the hot water and grated white chocolate. Sift the flour over the mixture and gently fold through until just combined.

Beat the egg whites with a clean electric beater until soft peaks form. Using a large metal spoon, fold the egg whites through the chocolate mixture until just combined. Pour the mixture into the prepared pan and bake for 12–15 minutes, or until the roulade is golden brown and firm to the touch.

Put a large sheet of baking paper on a flat surface and sprinkle with superfine sugar. Turn the roulade out onto the sugared paper. Trim any crisp edges and roll up from the short end with the aid of the baking paper. Set aside for 5 minutes, then unroll and leave to cool.

Meanwhile, put the berries in a bowl and sweeten them with superfine sugar, to taste. Beat the cream, confectioners' sugar, and vanilla until firm peaks form. Spread the roulade with the cream and sprinkle the berries over the top. Roll up and dust with confectioners' sugar. Cut into slices to serve.

Use the baking paper to help roll up the roulade.

Sprinkle the berries evenly over the cream.

peach and rosewater sorbet...................serves 4–6

THE BEAUTY OF SORBETS IS THAT THEY ARE EASY TO MAKE: THEY REQUIRE FEW INGREDIENTS AND NO SPECIAL EQUIPMENT. ALL THAT IS NEEDED IS THE TIME TO FREEZE AND WHISK THE SORBET THOROUGHLY. THIS SWEETLY SCENTED AND FLAVORED SORBET CAN BE DECORATED WITH UNSPRAYED ROSE PETALS.

peach tea	1²/₃ cups
superfine sugar	1¹/₃ cups
peaches	6
rose water	¹/₃ cup

Pour half the peach tea into a small saucepan. Add the sugar and stir until the sugar has dissolved. Bring to a boil and cook for 2 minutes, then remove from heat and set aside to cool.

Quarter the peaches, removing the stones. Put the peaches and remaining peach tea in a saucepan and poach for 10 minutes. Remove the peaches with a slotted spoon, reserving the liquid, and peel off the skin. Set aside to cool.

Using a hand blender or small food processor, puree the peaches, poaching liquid, sugar syrup, and rose water until smooth. Pour the mixture into a plastic container and freeze for 1¹/₂ hours, or until the sides and base have frozen and the middle is a soft slush.

Using a food processor or hand blender, process until the mixture is evenly slushy. Repeat the freezing and processing at least twice, then freeze for another 30–60 minutes.

Rose water is an expensive flower water that is made by distilling the fragrance of rose petals, most commonly the damask rose. The technique has been known since ancient Egyptian times, but the use of rose water reached its most lavish heights in the sumptuous cooking of Persia around the tenth century AD. Its popularity spread across the Middle East to India and Europe and it is still used to flavor traditional dishes such as Turkish delight, baklava, and lassi, as well as to add a sweet fragrance to curries and rice dishes. Rose water should be used only sparingly; otherwise dishes can take on a cloying sweetness.

the perfect crepe

Crepes are made using a sweetened batter of flour, milk, melted butter, and eggs. At their simplest, they are eaten with a dusting of sugar and a squeeze of lemon, or they can be wrapped around a filling or soaked in a sauce. It's important to let the batter stand to allow the gluten in the flour to relax, thus allowing the maximum amount of liquid to be absorbed. Secondly, and perhaps most importantly, don't touch the crepe while the first side is cooking.

If making several crepes at once, stack them between sheets of baking paper, then either keep them warm in a low oven or store them in the refrigerator. They freeze well when wrapped first in foil and then plastic wrap.

To make perfect crepes, sift 1$\frac{1}{4}$ cups all-purpose flour, a pinch of salt, and 1 teaspoon sugar into a large bowl. Make a well in the center. Whisk together 3 eggs and 1$\frac{3}{4}$ cups milk. Slowly pour this mixture into the well in the dry ingredients, whisking constantly and gradually drawing in the flour. Whisk in $\frac{1}{3}$ cup melted unsalted butter, then pour the batter into a container with a pouring lip. The batter should be the consistency of light cream. Let the batter stand in the refrigerator for 30 minutes.

Heat a crepe pan or nonstick frying pan over medium heat. Brush with a little melted unsalted butter, then pour in enough batter to form a thin layer, tilting and swirling the pan so the batter evenly covers the base. Tip out any excess batter and fill in any holes as necessary. Cook for about 1 minute without touching, or until the edge of the crepe starts to lift and the underside is golden brown. Use a palette knife to loosen the edge, and shake the pan to ensure the crepe isn't stuck. Carefully slide the palette knife under the crepe and flip it over. Cook for another 20–30 seconds, then slide the crepe onto a plate. Continue with the remaining batter, adding a little extra melted butter between crepes if necessary. Makes about 12.

caramelized peach and
passion-fruit crumble . . . . serves 6

USING STORE-BOUGHT PIE PASTRY MAKES THIS CRUMBLE A WONDERFULLY QUICK RECIPE. CHOOSE A GOOD-QUALITY, BUTTERY ONE AND LET IT SIT FOR 20 MINUTES BEFORE ROLLING IT OUT, OR IT WILL CRACK AND BE DIFFICULT TO WORK WITH. THE CARAMELIZED PEACHES BRING A MELLOW RICHNESS TO THIS DESSERT.

store-bought pie pastry	11 ounces, or 1 quantity from page 134
all-purpose flour	2/3 cup
soft brown sugar	1/4 cup
unsalted butter	3 tablespoons, chilled and cubed
shredded dried coconut	1/4 cup
roasted skinned hazelnuts	2 tablespoons chopped
peaches	4, sliced
superfine sugar	1/3 cup
passion fruits	3

Preheat the oven to 400°F. Roll out the pastry to cover the base and side of an 8-inch, 1 1/2-inch-deep fluted pie pan. Place the pastry in the pan and prick the base. Line the pastry shell with a sheet of crumpled baking paper and pour in some baking beads or uncooked rice. Bake for 15 minutes, then remove the paper and beads and return to the oven for another 6–8 minutes. Set aside to cool. Reduce the oven to 350°F.

Using fingertips, combine the flour, brown sugar, and butter. Add the coconut and chopped hazelnuts. Set aside.

Heat a frying pan over high heat. Toss the peach slices in the superfine sugar. Turn the peaches into the frying pan and cook, moving them occasionally until they are evenly coated in caramel. Add the passion-fruit pulp and remove the pan from heat.

Spoon the peach mixture into the baked pastry and top with the hazelnut mixture. Bake the crumble for 20–25 minutes, or until the top is golden brown.

Gently combine the butter into the flour and sugar.

Add the passion-fruit pulp to the caramelized peaches.

Sprinkle the hazelnut crumble over the top of the pie.

cherry cheesecake

EACH LAYER OF THIS CHEESECAKE JUST GETS BETTER, FROM THE BUTTERY COOKIE BASE TO THE RICH, CREAMY MIDDLE, TO THE DELICIOUSLY JUICY CHERRY TOPPING. TO REMOVE THE STONES FROM THE CHERRIES, EITHER USE A CHERRY PITTER OR CUT THE FRUIT IN HALF WITH A SMALL KNIFE, THEN REMOVE THE STONES.

cherries	19 ounces, pitted and halved
superfine sugar	heaping $1/2$ cup
lemon juice	2 tablespoons
sweet shortbread cookies	7 ounces
unsalted butter	$1/3$ cup, melted
cream cheese	2 cups, softened
honey	heaping $1/3$ cup
natural vanilla extract	2 teaspoons
lemon	1, zest finely grated
eggs	4, at room temperature
heavy whipping cream	heaping $3/4$ cup

Put a scant $1/2$ cup of water in a saucepan with the cherries, sugar, and lemon juice. Bring to a boil, then reduce the heat to low. Cook, stirring occasionally and lightly pressing the cherries to crush them, for 12–15 minutes, or until the cherries are soft and there are 2–3 tablespoons of syrup left. Remove from the heat and set aside to cool.

Preheat the oven to 350°F. Lightly grease an $8^1/2$-inch springform cake pan and line the base with baking paper. Crush the cookies in a food processor until they form fine crumbs. Add the butter and process until combined. Press the mixture into the base of the prepared pan and freeze for 10 minutes. Cover the outside of the pan with strong foil to prevent any water seepage during cooking. Place the cake pan in a deep roasting pan.

Beat the cream cheese, honey, vanilla, and lemon zest until smooth. Add the eggs, one at a time, beating well after each addition. Stir in the cream. Pour the mixture over the crumb base. Pour enough hot water into the roasting pan to come halfway up the side of the cake pan. Bake for 45 minutes, or until almost set. Carefully spoon the cherry mixture over the cheesecake, lightly spreading it to the edge. Bake for 10 minutes, or until just set. Remove from the roasting pan, discard the foil, place the cheesecake on a wire rack to cool in the pan, then refrigerate until ready to serve. Allow the cheesecake to return to room temperature before serving.

Cook the cherries until they are soft and syrupy.

Pour in the filling once the base is cold.

Be gentle when spreading the cherries over the cheesecake.

vanilla buttermilk panna cotta
with summer fruits

. . . . serves 4

ITS NAME SEEMS TO SUGGEST OTHERWISE, BUT BUTTERMILK IS ACTUALLY MADE FROM SKIM MILK AND IS LOWER IN FAT THAN FULL-CREAM MILK. AN ACID-PRODUCING BACTERIA IS ADDED TO THE MILK, THICKENING IT AND GIVING IT A TANGY FLAVOR. IT GOES PERFECTLY IN THIS PANNA COTTA, PRODUCING A SMOOTH, CREAMY DESSERT.

panna cotta

powdered gelatin	2 teaspoons
light cream	1 cup
superfine sugar	1/4 cup
vanilla bean	1/2, split lengthwise
buttermilk	1 cup
passion fruits	2
superfine sugar	2 teaspoons
small pineapple	1/2, peeled and cored
small red papaya	1/2, seeded and peeled

To make the panna cotta, lightly grease four 1/2-cup metal, glass, or ceramic molds.

Put 2 teaspoons of water in a small bowl and sprinkle with the gelatin. Leave the gelatin to sponge and swell. Put the cream, sugar, and vanilla bean in a small saucepan and stir over low heat for 2–3 minutes, or until the sugar has dissolved. Whisk the gelatin mixture into the cream mixture until the gelatin has dissolved. Set aside to infuse for 3 minutes.

Scrape the seeds from the vanilla bean into the cream mixture, discarding the vanilla pod. Pour the mixture into a bowl. Shake the buttermilk carton well before measuring, then whisk the buttermilk into the cream mixture. Divide the mixture among the prepared molds. Put the molds on a tray, cover with plastic wrap, and refrigerate for 3–4 hours, or until set.

Sieve the passion-fruit pulp into a small bowl, discarding the seeds. Stir in the sugar. Cut the pineapple and papaya into long thin slivers.

To serve, gently run a small knife around the side of each mold and turn the panna cotta out onto large serving plates. If they don't readily come out, briefly dip the molds in a bowl of hot water. Arrange the fruit slivers around the panna cotta and drizzle with the passion-fruit juice.

Remove the papaya seeds using a spoon.

Divide the panna cotta mixture among the molds.

ricotta and berry tartlets · serves 6

RICOTTA IS A FRESH CHEESE THAT PROVES SURPRISINGLY ADAPTABLE IN THE KITCHEN. IN SWEET DISHES IT GOES WELL WITH CHOCOLATE, DRIED FRUIT, NUTS, AND BERRIES. IT MAKES A NICE ALTERNATIVE TO A FRANGIPANE-STYLE FILLING IN THESE TARTLETS AND ALSO PROTECTS THE FRUIT DURING COOKING, ENSURING A MOIST FILLING.

pastry

all-purpose flour	1¼ cups
ground almonds	⅓ cup
superfine sugar	1 tablespoon
unsalted butter	⅓ cup, chilled and cubed
salt	pinch
egg yolk	1, at room temperature

filling

mixed berries, such as raspberries, strawberries, and blueberries	2½ cups
egg	1, at room temperature
superfine sugar	¼ cup
lemon juice	1 tablespoon
smooth ricotta cheese	scant ⅔ cup
confectioners' sugar	for dusting

To make the pastry, put the flour, ground almonds, sugar, butter, and pinch of salt in a food processor. Process until the mixture resembles bread crumbs. Add the egg yolk and 1 tablespoon of cold water. Process until the mixture just forms a ball, adding a little extra water if the pastry is too dry. Turn the pastry out onto a work surface. Flatten it into a disk, cover with plastic wrap, and refrigerate for 30 minutes.

Lightly grease six 3½-inch, ¾-inch-deep tartlet pans. Roll out the pastry on a lightly floured surface to a thickness of ⅛ inch. Cut out six 5-inch circles and place in the pans. Prick the base of the pastry with a fork and refrigerate for 10 minutes. Preheat the oven to 400°F.

To make the filling, hull any strawberries and chop any larger berries. Put the egg, superfine sugar, and lemon juice in a heatproof bowl and place over a saucepan of simmering water, making sure the base of the bowl doesn't touch the water. Whisk with an electric beater for 5–6 minutes, or until light and creamy. Stir in the ricotta. Divide the berries among the pastry cases, then spoon the ricotta mixture over the top of the berries. Bake for 20–22 minutes, or until the edges of the pastry are golden brown. Serve warm or at room temperature, dusted with confectioners' sugar.

Hull the strawberries and chop any larger ones.

Make sure the base of the bowl doesn't touch the water.

Divide the berries evenly among the pastry cases.

autumn

If desserts can be said to help ease the passing of summer and the arrival of colder weather, then these autumn recipes are just the ones to do it. What is there to lament when figs, plums, blackberries, and pears start appearing in the fruit stands, and desserts such as fig and apple pies with rose-water cream, pear tarte tatin, and plum upside-down cake are possible? Autumn recipes, like the season itself, have their own pleasures.

This chapter contains some classic flavor combinations. Plums with almonds, blackberries with crème anglaise, and figs with hazelnuts and yogurt are no less delicious for their familiarity. But, like every season, autumn also has its own rare treasures. Pomegranates, native to Iran and favored by the ancient Persians and Egyptians, can be found in stores—big, round red fruit filled with little jewel-like capsules of pulp and seeds. These are the sort of exotic fruit you might tend to overlook, since you wonder what they taste like and how they should be prepared. Well, two suggestions are Turkish delight ice cream and fruit fritters with pomegranate sauce.

With the gradual dwindling of the fresh fruit selection, dried fruit becomes a useful standby. Dried fruit has its own concentrated sweetness and appealing texture to offer, and it is particularly at home in fruit fritters.

The recipes in this chapter also mark a welcome return of the sweet, sticky, and syrupy. Pistachio and lime semolina cake with date confit or crystallized ginger cheesecake with Sauternes-poached plums are desserts that encourage the licking of fingers, bowls, and spoons. Freshly baked cakes and pies, ganache logs, and strudels all seem very much at home during autumn.

This chapter also shows you how to make a really good pie pastry, one of the most indispensable techniques for anyone who enjoys baking. You can buy ready-made pie pastry, and some brands are good, but none can provide the satisfaction and taste that come with making your own.

turkish delight ice cream......................................serves 6

THIS SWEET, ROSE-HUED ICE CREAM WILL HAVE EVERYONE WONDERING WHAT THE SECRET ELEMENT IS. MAKE SURE YOU BUY A GOOD-QUALITY TURKISH DELIGHT. IF IT IS QUITE PALE, YOU CAN ADD A FEW DROPS OF RED FOOD COLORING TO THE MILK AFTER DISSOLVING THE TURKISH DELIGHT.

milk	1 1/2 cups
light cream	2 cups
superfine sugar	2/3 cup
egg yolks	6, at room temperature
Turkish delight	3 1/2 ounces, roughly chopped
pomegranate seeds	2 tablespoons

Put 1 cup of the milk in a saucepan with the cream and sugar. Cook over medium heat, stirring constantly for a few minutes, until the sugar has dissolved and the milk is just about to boil. Remove from heat.

Whisk the egg yolks in a bowl for 1 minute, or until combined, then add 1/4 cup of the hot milk mixture. Stir to combine, then pour into the remaining milk mixture. Return the saucepan to low–medium heat and cook, stirring constantly with a wooden spoon, until the mixture thickens and coats the back of the spoon. Do not allow the mixture to boil. Strain through a fine sieve and set aside to cool.

Put the remaining milk and the Turkish delight in a small saucepan over medium heat. Stir constantly until the Turkish delight has dissolved into the milk. Stir into the custard mixture and set aside to cool.

Transfer the mixture to an ice-cream machine to churn and freeze according to the manufacturer's instructions. Alternatively, transfer to a shallow tray and freeze, whisking every couple of hours until frozen to give the ice cream a creamy texture.

Serve the ice cream topped with the pomegranate seeds.

Add the chopped Turkish delight to the remaining milk.

Stir over gentle heat to dissolve the Turkish delight.

blackberry and pear strudel

serves 6–8

unsalted butter	1/2 cup
natural vanilla extract	1/2 teaspoon
pears	4, peeled, cored, and chopped
orange zest	1 teaspoon finely grated
lemon	1/2, juiced
phyllo pastry	5 sheets
fresh bread crumbs	1 1/2 cups
blackberries	1 1/2 cups
toasted flaked almonds	1/2 cup
golden raisins	1/2 cup
superfine sugar	3/4 cup
confectioners' sugar	for dusting
custard or vanilla ice cream	to serve

Preheat the oven to 350°F and line a baking sheet with baking paper. Melt 1/3 cup of the butter with the vanilla.

Melt the remaining butter in a frying pan and sauté the pears over low heat for 5 minutes, or until tender. Transfer to a large bowl with the orange zest and lemon juice. Toss lightly to combine.

Lay a sheet of phyllo pastry on a flat surface. Brush the melted butter over the pastry and sprinkle lightly with a fifth of the bread crumbs. Cover with another sheet of pastry and bread crumbs and repeat the process until you have used all the pastry. Sprinkle with the remaining fifth of the bread crumbs.

Add the blackberries, almonds, golden raisins, and superfine sugar to the pear mixture and toss gently to combine. Shape the filling into a log along one long edge of the pastry, leaving a 2-inch border. Fold in the sides, then roll up and place, seam side down, on the prepared baking sheet. Brush with the remaining melted butter and bake for 40 minutes, or until golden brown. Dust with confectioners' sugar and serve with custard or vanilla ice cream.

The pear is a risky fruit—when perfectly ripe, its juicy, mellow richness is hard to beat, but miss that brief moment and the downward slide will have already begun. The pear's versatility in cooking makes it worth the gamble, however. Pears can be used in sweet and savory dishes, eaten fresh in salads, or poached, pureed, baked, and sautéed. Available for much of the year, they are at their best, and in the greatest variety, during autumn. Popular choices include the soft and juicy Bosc pear; the slow-ripening, juicy Packham pear; and the aromatic Bartlett pear, which is ideal for cooking. When buying, choose smooth and firm but not hard pears.

brown sugar cream pots
with roasted plums . . . . serves 6

THESE CARAMELIZED PLUMS MAKE A WONDERFUL FOIL TO THE UNADULTERATED SWEET CREAMINESS OF THE CUSTARD POTS. VIN SANTO, MEANING "HOLY WINE," IS AN ITALIAN DESSERT WINE THAT IS SMOOTH, HIGH IN ALCOHOL, AND INTENSELY FLAVORED. IF YOU CANNOT FIND VIN SANTO, USE SWEET MARSALA.

cream pots

eggs	2, at room temperature
egg yolks	2, at room temperature
light cream	1 cup
natural vanilla extract	1 teaspoon
milk	1 cup
soft brown sugar	3/4 cup firmly packed
plums	6, halved, stones removed
Vin Santo	2 tablespoons
superfine sugar	1 tablespoon

Preheat the oven to 300°F.

Whisk the eggs, egg yolks, cream, and vanilla in a heatproof bowl until combined. Stir the milk and brown sugar in a small saucepan over low heat until the sugar has dissolved. Heat until almost boiling, then remove from heat. Add 1/4 cup of the hot milk to the egg mixture and whisk to combine, then whisk in the remaining milk mixture.

Strain the mixture into a container with a pouring lip and pour into six 1/2-cup ovenproof ramekins. Put the ramekins in a deep roasting pan and pour enough boiling water into the roasting pan to come halfway up the sides of the ramekins. Bake for 45 minutes, or until set. Set aside to cool for 30 minutes.

Meanwhile, increase the oven to 400°F. Arrange the plums on a baking sheet in a single layer, cut side up. Drizzle with the Vin Santo and sprinkle with the superfine sugar. Roast for 12 minutes, or until the plums soften and the skin blisters. Cool to room temperature, then serve alongside the cream pots.

Whisk the hot milk into the egg mixture until combined.

Drizzle the Vin Santo over the cut side of the plums.

Roast until the plums soften and the skin blisters.

fruit fritters with pomegranate sauce

THIS SOPHISTICATED DESSERT IS A FAR CRY FROM THE HUMBLE BANANA FRITTER WITH ICE CREAM. IN THIS VERSION, FRUIT AND NUTS ARE SOAKED IN RUM, WHILE THE BATTER INCORPORATES LEMON ZEST, VANILLA, AND WHITE WINE. TO FINISH, RUBY-RED POMEGRANATE SAUCE IS SET ASIDE TO BE DRIZZLED LUXURIANTLY OVER THE TOP.

apples	3
rum	1 tablespoon
toasted slivered almonds	1/3 cup
dried apricots	1/4 cup
raisins	1/3 cup
ground cinnamon	1/4 teaspoon
oil	for deep-frying
confectioners' sugar	for sprinkling

batter

all-purpose flour	1 3/4 cups
superfine sugar	2 tablespoons
dry white wine	1 cup
olive oil	1 tablespoon
lemon zest	1 teaspoon finely grated
natural vanilla extract	1 teaspoon
eggs	3, at room temperature, separated

sauce

sugar	1/3 cup
pomegranates	2
lemon juice	2 teaspoons

Peel, quarter, and core the apples, then thinly slice and roughly chop them. Put the apples in a large bowl and toss with the rum. Chop the almonds and apricots and add to the apples. Add the raisins and cinnamon and toss to combine. Set aside for 1 hour.

Meanwhile, to make the batter, sift the flour into a bowl and add the sugar. Gradually stir in the wine and olive oil. Add the lemon zest, vanilla, and egg yolks and beat to a smooth batter. Set aside in a cool place for 50 minutes.

To make the sauce, put the sugar and 1 cup of water in a small saucepan. Bring to a boil and cook for about 15 minutes, or until reduced by half. Scrape the seeds and squeeze the juice from the pomegranates into a bowl. Discard the white pith. Puree the pomegranate seeds and juice in a food processor, then pass the mixture through a coarse strainer. You should have about a scant 1/2 cup of liquid. Add the liquid and the lemon juice to the saucepan containing the sugar syrup and simmer for 5 minutes. Remove from heat and set aside.

Fold the apple mixture through the batter. Whisk the egg whites until stiff peaks form. Using a metal spoon, fold a large scoop of egg whites through the batter, then lightly fold the remaining egg whites through the batter.

Fill a deep fryer or medium saucepan one-third full with oil. Heat the oil to 315°F, or until a cube of bread dropped into the oil turns golden in 30 seconds. Carefully drop heaping tablespoons of the batter into the oil and fry for about 1 minute, or until golden. Remove with tongs and drain on paper towels.

Sprinkle the fritters with confectioners' sugar and serve immediately with the pomegranate sauce for drizzling over the top.

Add the zest, vanilla, and yolks, then beat to a smooth batter.

Make sure you don't include any of the white pith.

plum and biscotti ice cream . . . . serves 4

FOR THE GREATEST VISUAL IMPACT, USE LOVELY DARK-FLESHED BLOOD PLUMS, RATHER THAN YELLOW-FLESHED ONES. THE DARK VARIETIES TEND TO BE BETTER FOR COOKING. CHOP THE BISCOTTI THOROUGHLY—THEIR CRUNCHINESS SHOULD BE PART OF THE ICE CREAM, NOT A SEPARATE ELEMENT.

plums	1 pound
superfine sugar	1/3 cup
almond extract	a few drops
good-quality store-bought	2 cups
custard	
almond biscotti	2 3/4 ounces, chopped

Halve the plums, removing the stones. Combine the sugar and 1/2 cup water in a saucepan. Add the plums and poach for 10 minutes. Set aside to cool.

Puree the plums, poaching liquid, and almond extract until smooth. Carefully stir the plum mixture into the custard. Pour the mixture into a shallow plastic container and freeze for 1–1 1/2 hours, or until the sides and base have frozen and the center is a soft slush.

Using a hand blender or electric whisk, blend or beat the plum mixture until it is uniformly slushy. Return the mixture to the freezer, repeating the blending process at least twice.

Stir in the biscotti and freeze for another 30–60 minutes, or until the ice cream is firm.

After the heady rush of summer fruits, plums can sometimes struggle for attention, though undeservedly so. They are particularly valuable for cooks, who can use them in savory and sweet dishes, preserves, and jams. Plums are also excellent for poaching and stewing. Native to Europe and North America, there are over 2,000 varieties grown worldwide. The flesh can be yellow or dark purple, the flavor tart or sweet. Tart varieties, particularly the blood plums, are best used in cooking; sweeter and juicier ones should be enjoyed fresh. When buying plums, look for pleasantly scented fruit that yield slightly when pressed and have a whitish bloom on the skin.

pistachio and lime semolina cake with date glaze
.... serves 16

THIS CAKE TAKES ITS CUE FROM THE COOKING OF THE EASTERN MEDITERRANEAN, WHERE SEMOLINA-BASED CAKES AND PASTRIES ARE OFTEN SOAKED IN SWEET SYRUPS. DATES ARE A POPULAR CHOICE FOR SUCH SYRUPS, DUE TO THEIR HIGH SUGAR CONTENT. TO EASE THE RICHNESS OF THE SYRUP, LIME JUICE HAS BEEN ADDED.

date glaze

superfine sugar	heaping ³/4 cup
pitted dates	1¹/4 cups roughly chopped
limes	2, juiced
unsalted butter	¹/2 cup, softened
superfine sugar	heaping ¹/2 cup
limes	2, zest finely grated
eggs	2, at room temperature
fine semolina	3 cups
pistachio nuts	²/3 cup chopped
baking powder	2 teaspoons
baking soda	¹/2 teaspoon
plain yogurt	³/4 cup
milk	¹/2 cup
crème fraîche or heavy cream	to serve

To make the date glaze, put the sugar in a small saucepan with ³/4 cup water. Stir over medium heat until the sugar has dissolved. Add the dates and lime juice and bring to a boil. Reduce the heat and simmer for 6–8 minutes, or until the dates have softened. Remove from heat and set aside to cool.

Preheat the oven to 350°F. Grease the sides of a 9-inch square cake pan and line with the base with baking paper.

Put the butter, sugar, and lime zest in a large bowl and beat with an electric beater until light and fluffy. Add the eggs, one at a time, beating well after each addition. In a separate bowl, combine the semolina, pistachios, baking powder, and baking soda. Stir the semolina mixture and yogurt alternately through the butter mixture, then stir in the milk. Pour the mixture into the prepared pan and bake for 40 minutes, or until a skewer comes out clean when inserted into the center of the cake.

Spoon the date glaze over the hot cake in the pan and place on a wire rack to cool. Serve the cake warm or at room temperature, accompanied by crème fraîche or heavy cream.

Cook the chopped dates until they soften.

Mix the chopped pistachio nuts into the semolina.

Stir the semolina mixture and yogurt into the butter mixture.

fig and apple pies
with rosewater cream

THESE LITTLE PIES ARE A REAL CELEBRATION OF AUTUMN, WITH FIGS, APPLES, CITRUS, CINNAMON, AND VANILLA
ALL COMBINING TO PRODUCE A VERY WARMING, COMFORTING FLAVOR—A WONDERFUL WAY TO END A MEAL.
THE PIES CAN BE PREPARED AHEAD OF TIME AND REFRIGERATED UNTIL IT IS TIME TO PUT THEM IN THE OVEN.

rosewater cream

heavy whipping cream	1/2 cup
rose water	2 teaspoons
superfine sugar	1 tablespoon
apples	3, peeled, cored, and cut into 3/4-inch cubes
figs	3 fresh or 6 semidried, cut into 3/4-inch cubes
unsalted butter	3 tablespoons
superfine sugar	1/4 cup
orange	1, zest grated
lemon	1, zest grated
lemon	1/2, juiced
cinnamon stick	1
natural vanilla extract	1 teaspoon
store-bought pie pastry	1 sheet
egg white	1, at room temperature, beaten

To make the rosewater cream, beat the cream, rose water, and sugar in a bowl until thick. Refrigerate until needed.

Put the apples, figs, butter, sugar, orange zest, lemon zest, lemon juice, cinnamon stick, vanilla, and 2 tablespoons water in a saucepan. Stir over high heat until the butter has melted and the sugar has dissolved. Bring to a boil, then reduce the heat and simmer for 10 minutes, or until the apple is soft. Remove from the heat and set aside to cool.

Preheat the oven to 350°F and lightly grease four 1/2-cup ovenproof ramekins.

Pour the cooled apple mixture into the ramekins, discarding the cinnamon stick. Cut out four rounds of pastry 1/2 inch wider than the diameter of the ramekins. Lay the pastry rounds over the ramekins, pressing around the rims to seal. Brush the pastry with the egg white. Bake the pies for 40 minutes, or until golden brown. Serve warm with the rosewater cream.

Figs have been found among the funerary treasures in ancient Egyptian tombs, they grew in the Hanging Gardens of Babylon, were regarded as a symbol of fertility by the ancient Greeks, and appeared in the Bible. All in all, figs have long been held in high regard. Small, soft, and pear-shaped, varying in color from pale green to purple, the fruit has sweet, pulpy flesh full of tiny edible seeds. In cooking, figs are poached, broiled, added to pies, and preserved. The stems should always be removed before cooking. When buying, select firm, unblemished fruits that yield to gentle pressure. Figs are also sold semidried and dried.

three ways with almonds

ALMONDS ARE OFTEN IN THE BACKGROUND, A SUPPORTING FLAVOR ONLY, SO IT'S NICE TO SEE THEM SHINE IN THEIR OWN RIGHT OCCASIONALLY. FOR THE BEST FLAVOR, PREPARE ALMONDS YOURSELF. TO BLANCH, POUR BOILING WATER OVER THE NUTS, SOAK FOR 2 MINUTES, THEN SLIP THE SKINS OFF WITH YOUR FINGERS. CHOP THE NUTS WHILE THEY ARE STILL WARM. TO ROAST, PUT THE NUTS ON A TRAY AND COOK FOR 8–10 MINUTES IN A 350°F OVEN, THEN GRIND IN A FOOD PROCESSOR OR USING A MORTAR AND PESTLE.

almond brownies

Melt 1 1/3 cups chopped bittersweet couverture chocolate in a heatproof bowl over a saucepan of simmering water. Remove from heat and set aside to cool for 5 minutes. Beat 1/2 cup softened unsalted butter and 1/2 cup superfine sugar with an electric beater for 10 minutes. Add 2 eggs, one at a time, beating until well combined. Sift together 2 tablespoons Dutch cocoa powder, 1/4 cup all-purpose flour, and 1/4 cup self-rising flour in a separate bowl. Stir the cocoa mixture into the butter mixture until combined. Stir in the melted chocolate. Pour the mixture into an 8-inch, 2-inch-deep square cake pan lined with baking paper and neatly arrange 1/2 cup blanched almonds over the surface. Bake in a preheated 325°F oven for 35 minutes. Set aside to cool in the pan for 5 minutes before transferring to a wire rack to cool completely. Cut the brownies into 1 1/2-inch squares and dust with cocoa powder. Makes 25.

caramelized almond pies

Roast 1/2 cup flaked almonds in a preheated 400°F oven for 7 minutes, or until golden. Put 1/4 cup unsalted butter, 1/3 cup firmly packed soft brown sugar, and 1/4 cup water in a frying pan and stir over low heat until the sugar has dissolved. Stir in the almonds, then divide the mixture among four 3 1/2-inch greased, loose-bottomed pie pans. Thaw 1 sheet of frozen puff pastry and cut it into four 3 1/2-inch rounds. Place the pastry rounds on the tops of the pie pans and bake for 10 minutes, or until puffed and golden. Immediately turn the pies out of the pans so the pastry is on the bottom. Set aside to cool. Serves 4.

almond and lime puddings

Put 1/2 cup superfine sugar, 1 1/2 tablespoons unsalted butter, and 1/4 cup lime juice in a small saucepan. Stir over low heat until the sugar has dissolved. Bring to a simmer, then cook, without stirring, for 3 minutes, or until syrupy. Divide the syrup among four 2/3-cup ovenproof bowls. Sift 1 cup confectioners' sugar, 1/2 cup all-purpose flour, and 1/4 teaspoon baking powder into a bowl and stir in 2/3 cup ground almonds. Add 3 egg whites, 1 teaspoon natural vanilla extract, 2 teaspoons finely grated lime zest, and 1/3 cup melted unsalted butter and stir to combine. Divide the mixture among the bowls. Bake the puddings in a preheated 315°F oven for 20–22 minutes, or until golden. Set aside to cool for 10 minutes before serving warm with heavy cream. Serves 4.

almond brownies

plum and almond pie .... serves 8

THE PLEASURE IN THIS PIE IS AS MUCH IN THE MAKING AS IN THE EATING. IT DOESN'T MATTER IF YOUR PASTRY IS NOT FLAWLESSLY BUTTERY AND SMOOTH, OR YOUR PLUMS AREN'T PERFECTLY PLACED; THE RESULT WILL BE THE SAME—A DELICIOUS COMBINATION OF FRUIT AND NUTS.

pastry

all-purpose flour	1 1/2 cups
unsalted butter	scant 3/4 cup, chilled and cubed
superfine sugar	1/4 cup
sour cream	1 tablespoon

filling

unsalted butter	heaping 1/2 cup, softened
superfine sugar	1/2 cup
eggs	2, at room temperature
ground almonds	1 cup
all-purpose flour	2 tablespoons
plums	8–10, halved, stones removed
cream or ice cream	to serve

To make the pastry, put the flour, butter, and sugar in a food processor and process in short bursts until the mixture resembles fine bread crumbs. Add the sour cream and process in short bursts until the mixture comes together in a ball. Cover with plastic wrap and refrigerate for 20 minutes.

Preheat the oven to 400°F and grease a 9-inch, 3/4-inch-deep loose-bottomed pie pan.

Roll out the pastry to a thickness of 1/8 inch and use it to line the pan. Prick the pastry base with a fork and refrigerate for 30 minutes. Line the pastry shell with a sheet of crumpled baking paper and pour in some baking beads or uncooked rice. Bake for 15 minutes, remove the paper and beads, and return to the oven for another 5–7 minutes to ensure the pastry is crisp. Set aside to cool. Reduce the oven to 350°F.

To make the filling, cream the butter and sugar with an electric beater until light and fluffy. Add the eggs, one at a time, beating well after each addition. Fold in the ground almonds and flour. Spread the almond mixture over the base of the piecrust and top with the plum halves, cut side down. Bake for 25–30 minutes, or until the filling is set and golden. Serve the pie warm or at room temperature with cream or ice cream.

Add the ground almonds after the eggs have been incorporated.

Spread the filling evenly into the piecrust.

Arrange the plums, cut side down, on the almond filling.

chocolate ganache log .... serves 8–10

A GANACHE IS BASICALLY A FOOLISHLY RICH FROSTING MADE OF CHOCOLATE AND CREAM. THE TWO ARE HEATED UNTIL THE CHOCOLATE HAS MELTED, THEN THE MIXTURE IS COOLED AND SPREAD OVER A CAKE. THIS DESSERT IS NOTHING IF NOT INDULGENT, AND DESERVES TO BE APPROACHED WITH GUSTO.

cake

unsalted butter	heaping ³/₄ cup, softened
superfine sugar	²/₃ cup
eggs	6, at room temperature, separated
ground almonds	1 ¹/₄ cups
good-quality bittersweet chocolate	1 cup chopped, melted

ganache

light cream	scant ²/₃ cup
good-quality bittersweet chocolate	1 ¹/₂ cups chopped
instant coffee granules	2 teaspoons

To make the cake, preheat the oven to 350°F. Grease the sides of a 10 x 12-inch jelly-roll pan and line the base with baking paper.

Beat the butter and sugar with an electric beater until light and fluffy. Add the egg yolks, one at a time, beating well after each addition. Stir in the ground almonds and melted chocolate. Beat the egg whites in a separate bowl until stiff peaks form, then gently fold into the chocolate mixture.

Spread the mixture into the prepared pan and bake for 15 minutes. Reduce the oven to 315°F and bake for another 30–35 minutes, or until a skewer comes out clean when inserted into the center of the cake. Turn the cake onto a wire rack to cool.

To make the ganache, put the cream and chopped chocolate in a heatproof bowl over a small saucepan of barely simmering water, making sure the base of the bowl doesn't touch the water. Stir occasionally until the mixture is melted and combined. Stir in the coffee until it has dissolved. Remove from heat and set aside to cool for 2 hours, or until thickened to a spreading consistency.

Cut the cake lengthwise into three even pieces. Place a piece of cake on a serving plate and spread with a layer of ganache. Top with another layer of cake and another layer of ganache, followed by the remaining cake. Refrigerate for 30 minutes to set slightly. Cover the top and sides of the log with the remaining ganache and refrigerate for 3 hours, or preferably overnight.

Stir the ground almonds and chocolate into the cake mixture.

Spread the batter evenly into the prepared pan.

baked yogurt pie with figs and hazelnuts

UNLIKE MANY PIES THAT USE NUTS, BUTTER, AND FLOUR FOR THEIR FILLING, THIS MEDITERRANEAN-INSPIRED RECIPE FEATURES YOGURT AND A HIGHER PROPORTION OF EGGS THAN NORMAL TO ENSURE A MOIST, SMOOTH TEXTURE. THE SLIGHTLY SHARP FLAVOR OF THE FILLING IS THE IDEAL CONTRAST TO THE RICH, SWEET FIGS.

pastry

all-purpose flour	1 1/4 cups
ground hazelnuts	3/4 cup
unsalted butter	1/3 cup, cubed
salt	pinch
egg yolk	1, at room temperature

filling

eggs	3, at room temperature
egg yolks	2, at room temperature
superfine sugar	heaping 1/2 cup
vanilla beans	2, split lengthwise
plain yogurt	heaping 3/4 cup
cornstarch	1/4 cup
all-purpose flour	1/4 cup
figs	7, sliced
roasted skinned hazelnuts	heaping 3/4 cup roughly chopped
whipped cream	to serve

To make the pastry, put the flour, ground hazelnuts, butter, and pinch of salt in a food processor and process until the mixture resembles bread crumbs. Add the egg yolk and 1 tablespoon of cold water. Process until the mixture just forms a ball, adding a little extra water if the dough is too dry. Turn out onto a work surface and flatten into a disk. Cover with plastic wrap and refrigerate for 30 minutes.

Preheat the oven to 350°F. Lightly grease a 9-inch shallow fluted pie pan. Roll out the pastry on a lightly floured surface until 1/8 inch thick. Carefully transfer the pastry into the pan, prick the base with a fork, and refrigerate for 10 minutes. Roll a rolling pin across the top of the pie pan to remove any excess pastry.

To make the filling, beat the eggs, egg yolks, and sugar in a bowl until the sugar has dissolved. Scrape the seeds from the vanilla beans into the egg mixture and stir in the yogurt. Combine the cornstarch and flour and lightly fold through the yogurt mixture. Pour into the piecrust and top with the sliced figs and chopped hazelnuts. Bake for 18–20 minutes, or until just set. Leave the pie to cool in the pan, then remove and serve at room temperature. Serve with whipped cream.

Beat the eggs and sugar together until the sugar dissolves.

Pour the yogurt filling into the piecrust.

Arrange the sliced figs and hazelnuts on top of the filling.

plum upside-down cake . . . . serves 8

INVERTING A CAKE ALWAYS HAS A CERTAIN SENSE OF DRAMA TO IT—THAT MOMENT OF ANTICIPATION BEFORE YOU
SEE HOW IT TURNED OUT. IF YOU ARE HAVING TROUBLE REMOVING THE PLUM FLESH FROM THE STONES, SIMPLY
CUT IT AWAY IN SEGMENTS.

plums	1 pound
dark brown sugar	¼ cup
unsalted butter	heaping ⅓ cup, softened
superfine sugar	1 heaping cup
eggs	4, at room temperature
natural vanilla extract	1 teaspoon
orange	1, zest grated
cardamom pods	6, seeds removed and crushed
all-purpose flour	1¼ cups
ground almonds	1½ cups
baking powder	2 teaspoons
heavy cream	to serve

Preheat the oven to 350°F, and grease the sides of a 9-inch spring-form cake pan and line the base with baking paper.

Halve the plums, removing the stones. Sprinkle the brown sugar over the base of the prepared pan and arrange the plums, cut side down, over the sugar.

Cream the butter and superfine sugar with an electric beater until light and fluffy. Add the eggs, one at a time, beating well after each addition. Add the vanilla, orange zest, crushed cardamom seeds, flour, ground almonds, and baking powder. Spoon over the plums and smooth the surface with a spatula.

Bake for 50 minutes, or until a skewer comes out clean when inserted into the center of the cake. Set aside to cool for 5 minutes before turning the cake out onto a plate. Serve with heavy cream.

Like many spices, cardamom retains the appeal of the exotic though it is now readily available. Chewed by ancient Egyptians as a breath freshener, and introduced to Scandinavia by Viking traders, the plant is, in fact, native to India and Sri Lanka. The pods, the plant's dried fruit, contain the prized seeds: pungent and aromatic with a warm, sweet flavor. Beware of "false" cardamoms: the Indian green pods are the ones to buy. Not surprisingly, Indian cooks make good use of cardamom, though the spice is also much used in the Middle East, especially as a flavoring for coffee. The pods can be used whole, and the seeds whole or ground.

milk chocolate and pecan ice cream .... serves 6–8

A CREAMY CHOCOLATE ICE CREAM DOESN'T REALLY NEED ANY MORE CHOCOLATE, BUT THESE CURLS ARE DECORATIVE AND FUN TO MAKE, SO WHY NOT? IF YOU GET A BIT CARRIED AWAY AND FIND YOU HAVE MORE CURLS THAN YOU NEED, YOU CAN STORE THEM IN AN AIRTIGHT CONTAINER—OR, OF COURSE, EAT THEM!

milk	1/2 cup
vanilla bean	1, split lengthwise
heavy whipping cream	1 1/2 cups
superfine sugar	heaping 1/3 cup
milk chocolate	1 cup grated
egg yolks	2, at room temperature
pecans	1/2 cup, chopped
good-quality bittersweet chocolate	5 1/2-ounce block

Put the milk in a heavy-based saucepan. Scrape the seeds from the vanilla bean into the saucepan and add the pod. Add 1/2 cup of the cream and heat gently until just below the boiling point. Add the sugar and grated milk chocolate and stir, without boiling, until smooth.

Put the egg yolks in a heatproof bowl and beat to combine. Add the cream mixture, stirring constantly. Place the bowl over a saucepan of simmering water, making sure the base of the bowl doesn't touch the water. Stir for about 20 minutes, or until the custard is thick enough to coat the back of a spoon. Strain the custard into a 3-cup plastic or metal container and chill for 30 minutes.

Whip the remaining cream until soft peaks form, then fold the cream through the custard. Freeze for 1 1/2–2 hours, or until the ice cream starts to set. Whisk well with an electric beater to break up the ice crystals, then return to the freezer until the ice cream begins to freeze. Beat well, then stir in the pecans. Freeze until the ice cream is set.

Scrape a vegetable peeler along the chocolate block to make bittersweet chocolate curls. Set aside until ready to serve.

Transfer the ice cream to the refrigerator 5–10 minutes before serving. Scoop the ice cream into serving bowls and top with the chocolate curls.

Stir the chocolate and sugar into the cream until smooth.

Use a vegetable peeler to make chocolate curls.

steamed blackberry puddings with crème anglaise .... serves 8

THE KEY TO A SILKY-SMOOTH CRÈME ANGLAISE IS PATIENCE, AND THESE COMFORTING PUDDINGS PROVIDE A GOOD OPPORTUNITY TO PRACTICE. SLOWLY WHISK THE MILK INTO THE EGG YOLKS, AND SLOWLY COOK THE CUSTARD OVER LOW HEAT. WHEN DONE, SET THE CUSTARD OVER A BOWL OF ICED WATER TO PREVENT FURTHER COOKING.

unsalted butter	heaping 1/2 cup, softened
superfine sugar	heaping 1/2 cup
eggs	2, at room temperature
self-rising flour	1 cup, sifted
milk	2 tablespoons
blackberries	2 1/4 cups

crème anglaise

milk	1 1/3 cups
egg yolks	4, at room temperature
superfine sugar	1/3 cup

Preheat the oven to 350°F and grease eight 1/2-cup dariole molds.

Using an electric beater, cream the butter and sugar together until light and fluffy. Add the eggs, one at time, beating well after each addition. Gently fold in the sifted flour and enough milk to form a dropping consistency.

Cover the base of each of the prepared molds with a layer of blackberries. Spoon enough of the pudding mixture over the berries so that the molds are three-quarters full. Cover the molds with foil, sealing tightly. Place the steamed puddings in a roasting pan and pour in enough hot water to come halfway up the sides of the molds. Bake for 30–35 minutes, or until the puddings spring back when lightly touched.

Meanwhile, to make the crème anglaise, heat the milk to just below the boiling point, then set aside. Beat the egg yolks and sugar with an electric beater until thick and pale. Slowly whisk in the hot milk and pour the mixture into a saucepan. Cook over low heat, stirring constantly for 5–7 minutes, or until the custard is thick enough to coat the back of a spoon. Remove from heat.

To serve, unmold the puddings onto plates and drizzle with the crème anglaise.

Only fill the dariole molds three-quarters full.

Pour hot water into the roasting pan around the molds.

passion-fruit polenta cake

serves 8–10

POLENTA, MADE FROM CORNMEAL, ADDS A WONDERFUL GOLDEN HUE TO THIS CAKE. COMBINED WITH THE FLOUR AND ALMONDS, IT PROVIDES A GOOD CONTRAST FOR THE SHARPER CITRUS AND PASSION-FRUIT FLAVORS. YOU WILL NEED ABOUT SIX LARGE PASSION FRUITS FOR THIS RECIPE.

eggs	6, at room temperature, separated
superfine sugar	2/3 cup
oranges	2, zest grated
passion-fruit pulp (flesh and seeds)	1/2 cup
natural vanilla extract	2 teaspoons
toasted slivered almonds	1 1/4 cups
fine polenta	1 cup
self-rising flour	1 1/4 cups
whipped cream	to serve

syrup

passion fruits	2
oranges	2, zested and juiced
orange-blossom honey	1/4 cup

whiskey butter sauce

honey	1/4 cup
whiskey	1/4 cup
unsalted butter	3 tablespoons, chilled and cubed

Preheat the oven to 325°F and grease a 9 1/2-inch springform cake pan.

Whisk the egg whites in a large bowl until stiff peaks form. Beat the egg yolks and sugar in a separate bowl for 3–4 minutes, or until smooth and pale. Add the orange zest, passion-fruit pulp, and vanilla and beat for 15 seconds, or until smooth.

Put the almonds in a food processor and process until finely ground. Add the polenta and flour and process in short bursts until combined.

Using a metal spoon, lightly fold a large scoop of egg whites through the passion-fruit mixture, then gently fold the passion fruit–egg mixture through the remaining egg whites. Fold in the almond mixture and spoon into the prepared pan. Bake for 30–35 minutes, or until a skewer inserted into the center of the cake comes out hot and clean. Set aside to cool for 15 minutes, then turn out onto a wire rack to cool for at least 1 hour.

To make the syrup, cut the passion fruits in half and scoop out the flesh and edible seeds. Put the orange zest, orange juice, passion-fruit pulp (flesh and seeds), and honey in a small saucepan. Bring to a boil over medium heat, then reduce heat and simmer for 5 minutes.

Transfer the cake to a serving plate with a lip, and pierce it several times with a thin metal skewer. Pour about one-quarter of the hot syrup all over the top, then add the rest once it is absorbed. Set aside for 1 hour.

To make the whiskey butter sauce, put the honey and whiskey in a saucepan and bring to a boil over low–medium heat. Reduce heat and simmer for 1 minute, then gradually add the butter, one cube at a time, waiting for each cube to melt before adding the next.

Serve the cake cut into wedges, with lightly whipped cream and the whiskey butter sauce.

Don't knock out the air when folding in the passion-fruit mixture.

Allow the syrup to be absorbed before adding more.

the perfect
pie pastry

Pie pastry is made using flour, fat, and water and can be enriched with egg yolk to make a pastry that is softer and not as crisp. It's important to use just enough liquid to hold the pastry together—too wet, and it may toughen and shrink on baking; too dry, and it will be crumbly.

The secret to the perfect pie pastry is to work quickly and lightly, with cool ingredients in a cool room. A cold marble slab is the ideal work surface, but if you don't have one, try resting a tray of ice cubes on your work surface for a few minutes before you start.

Sift 1½ cups all-purpose flour into a large bowl and add a heaping ⅓ cup chilled, cubed, unsalted butter. Using your fingertips, rub the butter into the flour until the mixture is crumblike. Make a well in the center, add 2–4 tablespoons of cold water, and use a flat-bladed knife to mix to a soft, but not sticky, dough. Use a cutting rather than a stirring motion and turn the bowl with your free hand. To test if the dough needs more water, pinch a little dough between your fingers—if it doesn't hold together, add a little more water.

Gently gather the dough together and transfer to a floured work surface or sheet of baking paper. Gently press the dough into a ball, using a few light actions. Press into a flat disk, wrap in plastic, and refrigerate for 20 minutes.

Roll out the pastry on a lightly floured work surface or between two sheets of baking paper, rolling from the center outward and rotating the pastry, rather than rolling backward and forward. If rolling on a work surface, roll the pastry around the rolling pin and lift it into the pan. If using baking paper, peel off the top sheet, then carefully invert the pastry over the pan, making sure it is centered, and peel off the bottom sheet of paper. Once the pastry is in the pan, quickly lift up the sides so they don't break on the edges of the pan. Gently ease and press the pastry into the pan. Refrigerate for at least 15 minutes to relax the pastry to prevent or minimize shrinkage, then roll a rolling pin across the top of the pan to cut off any excess pastry. Makes enough pastry to line a 9-inch pan.

black and white chocolate pie.....................serves 12

THIS DECADENT DESSERT IS UNDOUBTEDLY ONE FOR SPECIAL OCCASIONS. HAPPILY, THE BULK OF THE WORK MUST
BE DONE THE DAY BEFORE THE TART IS NEEDED, WHICH WILL FORCE YOU TO BE WELL PREPARED! RICH, CREAMY,
AND SUPER CHOCOLATY, IT MIGHT BE WISE TO SERVE THIS PIE WITH COFFEE.

pastry

unsalted butter	scant 1/3 cup, at room temperature
superfine sugar	1/4 cup
egg	1, at room temperature, lightly beaten
all-purpose flour	1 1/2 cups
self-rising flour	1/4 cup
cocoa powder	1 tablespoon

filling

gelatin	2 teaspoons powdered
milk	heaping 3/4 cup
superfine sugar	1/2 cup
good-quality white chocolate	1/2 cup chopped
egg yolks	4, at room temperature, lightly beaten
light cream	1 cup, whipped to soft peaks

chocolate glaze

light cream	1/4 cup
good-quality bittersweet chocolate	1/2 cup chopped
unsalted butter	2 teaspoons, cubed
light corn syrup	2 teaspoons

Preheat the oven to 375°F. Lightly grease the sides of an 8-inch springform cake pan and line the base with baking paper.

To make the pastry, beat the butter with an electric beater until smooth and fluffy. Beat in the sugar and egg until combined. Sift in the combined flours and cocoa powder and stir until the dough comes together. Knead briefly on a lightly floured surface until smooth. Flatten into a disk, wrap in plastic wrap, and refrigerate for 30 minutes.

Roll the pastry between two sheets of baking paper until about 3/8 inch thick, and trim to fit the base of the prepared pan. Ease the pastry into the pan, removing the paper, and lightly prick with a fork. Bake for 15 minutes, or until slightly firm to touch. Set aside to cool.

To make the filling, put 2 tablespoons of water in a small bowl, sprinkle with the powdered gelatin, and set aside for 2 minutes to sponge and swell. Heat the milk, sugar, and chocolate in a saucepan until simmering. Stir until the sugar has dissolved and the chocolate has melted. Put the egg yolks in a bowl and whisk in the warm chocolate mixture. Return the mixture to a clean saucepan and stir over medium heat until it lightly coats the back of a spoon. Add the sponged gelatin to the saucepan and stir until the gelatin has dissolved. Transfer to a bowl, place over a bowl of ice, and beat until cold. Fold in the cream. Pour the mixture over the pastry and refrigerate overnight, or until set.

To make the chocolate glaze, put the cream, chocolate, butter, and corn syrup in a saucepan and stir over low–medium heat until smooth. Allow the glaze to cool slightly until thickened.

Remove the pie from the pan and spoon the glaze over the top, allowing it to drip down the side. Use a metal spatula to smooth the glaze over the top of the pie. Set aside at room temperature for 1 hour, or until the glaze is set.

crystallized ginger cheesecake
with sauternes-poached plums . . . . serves 8

THIS RECIPE OFFERS A SOPHISTICATED TWIST ON THE SMOOTH, RICH FLAVORS OF TRADITIONAL CHEESECAKES. IT IS STILL CREAMY, BUT HAS ADDED DEPTH FROM THE GINGERSNAP COOKIE BASE AND GINGER-TINGED FILLING. THE PLUMS PROVIDE YET ANOTHER LAYER OF FLAVOR AND TEXTURE—SWEET, FRUITY, AND GOLDEN.

gingersnaps	4$\frac{1}{2}$ ounces
unsalted butter	2 tablespoons, melted
powdered gelatin	2 teaspoons
boiling water	$\frac{1}{4}$ cup
cream cheese	2 cups
sweetened condensed milk	14-ounce can
crystallized ginger in syrup	2 pieces, chopped
crystallized ginger syrup	$\frac{1}{4}$ cup
plums	5
Sauternes	scant $\frac{1}{2}$ cup
superfine sugar	2 tablespoons

Put the gingersnaps in a food processor and process until they form fine crumbs. Transfer the crumbs to a bowl and combine with the melted butter. Spoon the mixture into an 8-inch springform cake pan, pressing firmly to make a base. Refrigerate for 30 minutes.

Dissolve the gelatin in the boiling water. Put the cream cheese, condensed milk, ginger, syrup, and the gelatin mixture in a food processor and process until smooth. Pour over the chilled base and refrigerate for 3 hours.

Halve the plums, removing the stones. Combine the Sauternes and sugar in a saucepan and add the plums in a single layer. Gently poach the plums for 4 minutes, then set aside to cool.

Arrange the plums, cut side up, on top of the cheesecake and drizzle with the poaching liquid.

A knobbly, brown rhizome from a tropical plant, ginger may not have the beauty of saffron or rose water, or the exotic charm of vanilla beans or cinnamon sticks, but it is just as indispensable in the kitchen as any of these. Its value lies not only in its lively and refreshing flavor and aroma but also in its medicinal properties. Ginger is indigenous to Southeast Asia, where it is used extensively in both savory and sweet dishes. However, it is hard to find a cuisine that doesn't make use of ginger. It is available fresh year-round, and is also sold dried, powdered, candied, and preserved in syrup as crystallized ginger.

passion-fruit mousse with red-grape syrup

serves 10

THE FLAVORS AND COLORS OF DESSERTS DON'T HAVE TO TURN SOMBER JUST BECAUSE IT'S AUTUMN. THIS RECIPE COMBINES THE LIVELY TANG OF A PASSION-FRUIT-FLAVORED MOUSSE WITH A SWEET RED-GRAPE SYRUP. YOU WILL NEED ABOUT 20 FRESH PASSION FRUITS OR TWO 6-OUNCE CANS OF PASSION-FRUIT PULP.

eggs	4, at room temperature, separated
superfine sugar	3/4 cup, plus 2 tablespoons
passion-fruit juice	3/4 cup, strained
powdered gelatin	2 tablespoons
hot water	1/4 cup
heavy whipping cream	1 1/4 cups
cherry brandy, such as Kirsch	1/4 cup
natural vanilla extract	1 teaspoon
seedless red grapes	1 1/3 cups

Put the egg yolks and 3/4 cup of the sugar in a heatproof bowl and whisk with an electric beater until thick and pale. Stir in the passion-fruit juice. Place the bowl over a saucepan of simmering water, making sure the base of the bowl doesn't touch the water. Stir for 6–8 minutes, or until the mixture is thick enough to coat the back of a wooden spoon.

Dissolve the gelatin in the hot water and add it to the passion-fruit mixture. Set aside to cool.

Whip the cream until soft peaks form. In a separate bowl, beat the egg whites until soft peaks form. Gently fold the cream and egg whites through the passion-fruit mixture. Pour into ten 1/2-cup molds and refrigerate for 4 hours, or until set.

Meanwhile, put 1/2 cup water, the cherry brandy, the remaining 2 tablespoons of sugar, and the vanilla in a small saucepan. Stir over low heat until the sugar has dissolved, then increase the heat and simmer for 12 minutes. Remove from heat, add the grapes, and set aside to cool.

To serve, dip the base of each mold in hot water for 5 seconds and invert the mousse onto a plate. Accompany with the grapes and a little syrup.

Stir the passion-fruit juice into the sugar and eggs.

Cook the custard gently until it coats the back of the spoon.

Divide the passion-fruit mixture among the molds.

pear tarte tatin

THIS DESSERT IS JUSTIFIABLY A CLASSIC—IT IS VERY EASY TO MAKE AND LOOKS AND TASTES GREAT. IF YOU CAN, USE SMALL PEARS WITH GREEN SKIN AND A PINK BLUSH. YOU ALSO NEED PEARS WITH FIRM, WHITE FLESH WITH A RICH LUSHNESS TO IT. GOOD VARIETIES TO USE ARE PACKHAM AND BOSC.

unsalted butter	1/4 cup, chopped
raw superfine sugar	heaping 1/3 cup
pears	5
pecans	9
frozen puff pastry	2 sheets, thawed
cream or vanilla ice cream	to serve

Put the butter and sugar in an 8-inch tarte tatin pan or heavy-based frying pan with an ovenproof handle. Heat gently, without stirring, for 1 minute, or until the sugar has caramelized and turned golden brown. Don't worry if the butter separates at this stage. Remove from heat.

Peel, halve, and core the pears, leaving the stalks intact. Arrange the pears, cut side up, in a circle over the caramel, with the stalks toward the center. Place one pear half in the center, and fill in the gaps with the pecans. Cover and cook the pears over low heat for 20 minutes, or until tender.

Preheat the oven to 375°F. Lay one sheet of pastry on top of the other and roll firmly and evenly so that they stick together and increase in size by 1/2–3/4 inches. Trim the pastry to a circle 1 inch larger than the upper rim of the pan and place over the pears. Gently push the edges of the pastry down between the pears and the pan.

Bake for 20 minutes, or until golden. Carefully drain the sauce from the pan into a small saucepan and simmer for 4–5 minutes, or until reduced and syrupy. Turn the tarte tartin out onto a serving plate and pour the reduced sauce over the top. Serve immediately with cream or vanilla ice cream.

Arrange the pears, cut side up, in the pan.

Lay the pastry over the pears and tuck the edge down the side.

winter

There are no half measures in winter; instead, there are layers upon layers of everything that is rich and satisfying. Gooey chocolate desserts come with a chocolate sauce, and chocolate, hazelnut, and orange dessert cake is served with a blood-orange sauce. The colors are deep and golden, the tastes and textures wonderfully warm, sweet, and indulgent. Pity the brave person who decides to diet this winter! For, while it is true that apple and passion-fruit crumble and almond and rosewater puddings with orange and date salad manage to avoid chocolate and cream—even the hedonists among us need the occasional change of pace—these light offerings are not the real focus of this chapter. Instead, most of the recipes here seem to have but one goal: to make sure you and your guests finish a meal truly and gloriously satisfied.

Many of the recipes are very simple to make—almost comforting, such is the emphasis on gently melting chocolate, slowly caramelizing apples in butter and sugar, steadily folding through whipped cream. Similarly, the bulk of the ingredients are reassuringly familiar: eggs, cream, flour, almonds, vanilla, and chocolate—lots of it. Chocolate is the unchallenged star of this chapter, so it's worth buying a good-quality block, particularly when it is the key flavoring in a recipe. Look for chocolate with at least 50 percent cocoa liquor and that does not contain vegetable fats.

Most of us are happy to have chocolate with pretty much anything, but there are a few standout combinations that are hard to surpass—chocolate with liqueurs, with nuts such as hazelnuts and almonds, with spices such as cinnamon, and with fruit such as oranges. Winter also sees the arrival of kumquats and blood oranges, both visually dramatic ways to signal the season. Try honey parfait with caramelized kumquats, or topping a favorite dessert with a hot blood-orange and cardamom sauce. Don't forget, however, those old faithfuls, apples and bananas, which also excel during the colder months—recipes include banana fritters with butterscotch sauce and brioche with caramelized apples and crème anglaise. Like many of the desserts here featuring fruit, it's hard not to suspect that their primary purpose is to serve as a foil to a very good sauce: bananas with butterscotch, oranges with caramel, and strawberries with chocolate and liqueur.

brioche and butter pudding . . . . serves 8

IF THIS DOESN'T WARM YOU UP ON A COLD WINTER'S NIGHT, NOTHING WILL. BRIOCHE IS A LIGHT BUT RICH, BUTTERY BREAD; IF NOT AVAILABLE, TRY CRUSTY WHITE BREAD, CROISSANTS, OR EVEN PANETTONE. TO MAKE YOUR OWN CINNAMON SUGAR, COMBINE TWO PARTS SUPERFINE SUGAR WITH ONE PART GROUND CINNAMON.

dark corn syrup	2 tablespoons
brioche or crusty white bread	ten 3/4-inch thick slices
unsalted butter	3 tablespoons, softened
apricot jam	heaping 1/4 cup
eggs	4, at room temperature
sugar	heaping 1/3 cup
milk	heaping 3 cups
natural vanilla extract	1 teaspoon
cinnamon sugar	1/2 teaspoon

caramel sauce

unsalted butter	1/3 cup, chopped
soft brown sugar	1/3 cup
dark corn syrup	2 tablespoons
light cream	1 cup

Preheat the oven to 350°F and lightly grease a 9-cup-capacity ovenproof dish. Drizzle the corn syrup into the dish.

Spread the brioche slices with the butter and apricot jam and arrange in layers in the prepared dish.

Whisk the eggs, sugar, milk, and vanilla in a bowl until combined. Slowly pour the mixture over the brioche slices, allowing it to be absorbed gradually. Set aside for 10 minutes. Sprinkle with the cinnamon sugar and bake for 40 minutes, or until a knife comes out clean when inserted into the center of the pudding.

Meanwhile, to make the caramel sauce, put the butter, brown sugar, and corn syrup in a small saucepan and bring to a boil. Add the cream, reduce the heat, and simmer for 3–4 minutes.

Serve the caramel sauce poured over the warm pudding.

Obtaining vanilla is a labor-intensive and involved process, which helps explain why it is such an expensive flavoring. The pollination of the climbing orchid vine from which vanilla is obtained is intricate and occurs naturally only in its native Mexico. The resulting green beans are picked, dried, and fermented. This causes them to shrivel, turn deep brown, and acquire a light coating of white vanillin crystals, the source of the all-important flavor. Good-quality vanilla beans have a warm, caramel aroma and flavor and should be soft, not hard and dry. Vanilla is also sold distilled into natural vanilla extract—beware of cheap imitations.

banana fritters
with butterscotch sauce .... serves 4

IT'S EASY TO SEE WHY THIS FABULOUS DESSERT IS A CHILDHOOD FAVORITE—MELTING BANANA IN A CRISPY, HOT CASING WITH SMOOTH, GOLDEN BUTTERSCOTCH SAUCE. THE WARM BANANA SMELLS WONDERFUL TOO, ADDING TO THE PLEASURE. YOU CAN STORE ANY LEFTOVER SAUCE IN THE REFRIGERATOR FOR UP TO 2 WEEKS.

butterscotch sauce

unsalted butter	1/4 cup
dark corn syrup	1/3 cup
soft brown sugar	1/3 cup
superfine sugar	1/4 cup
light cream	2/3 cup
natural vanilla extract	1/2 teaspoon

batter

self-rising flour	1 cup
egg	1, at room temperature, beaten
club soda	3/4 cup
unsalted butter	1 1/2 tablespoons, melted

oil	for deep-frying
firm bananas	4
confectioners' sugar	for dusting
ice cream	to serve

To make the butterscotch sauce, put the butter, corn syrup, brown sugar, and superfine sugar in a small saucepan. Stir over low heat for 2–3 minutes, or until the sugar has dissolved. Increase the heat a little and simmer for 3–5 minutes, taking care not to burn the sauce. Remove the pan from heat and stir in the cream and vanilla.

To make the batter, sift the flour into a bowl and make a well in the center. Add the egg and club soda and whisk until smooth. Whisk in the melted butter.

Fill a saucepan one-third full of oil and heat to 400°F, or until a cube of bread dropped into the oil browns in 5 seconds.

Cut each banana into thirds and add to the batter in batches. Use a spoon to coat the banana in the batter.

Using a slotted spoon, carefully lower the banana into the hot oil in batches. Cook each batch for 2–3 minutes, turning until the fritters are puffed and golden brown all over. Drain the fritters on paper towels.

Serve the fritters hot, dusted with confectioners' sugar. Accompany with ice cream and the butterscotch sauce.

Melt the butter, sugars, and corn syrup together.

Dip the pieces of banana into the batter in batches.

chocolate, almond, and cardamom cake

serves 8–10

THOUGH THIS CAKE COULD NOT BE EASIER TO MAKE, IT DOES NOT LACK FLAVOR. GROUND CARDAMOM, LIKE ANY SPICE, CAN LOSE ITS AROMATIC QUALITIES OVER TIME, SO BUY FROM A SPECIALTY SPICE STORE OR GRIND YOUR OWN. CRÈME FRAÎCHE HAS A SLIGHTLY NUTTY, SHARP FLAVOR, WHICH COMPLEMENTS THE SWEET CHOCOLATE.

good-quality bittersweet chocolate	$1^{2}/_{3}$ cups chopped
unsalted butter	1 cup, chopped
natural vanilla extract	1 teaspoon
hot water	1 cup
superfine sugar	$^{3}/_{4}$ cup
eggs	3, at room temperature, lightly beaten
self-rising flour	$1^{1}/_{3}$ cups, sifted
ground almonds	1 cup
ground cardamom	3 teaspoons
confectioners' sugar	$^{1}/_{4}$ cup
crème fraîche or whipped cream	to serve

Preheat the oven to 315°F. Grease the sides of a $9^{1}/_{2}$-inch springform cake pan and line with baking paper.

Put the chocolate, butter, vanilla, and hot water in a heatproof bowl. Sit the bowl over a saucepan of barely simmering water, making sure the base of the bowl doesn't touch the water. Heat gently until the chocolate has melted. Remove from heat and stir in the superfine sugar. Add the eggs and beat well to combine.

Combine the sifted flour, ground almonds, and 2 teaspoons of the cardamom and fold through the chocolate mixture, beating well to combine. Pour the mixture into the prepared pan and bake for 40 minutes, or until a skewer inserted into the center of the cake comes out almost clean. Set aside in the pan for 10 minutes, then turn out onto a wire rack to cool.

Combine the remaining cardamom with the confectioners' sugar and dust over the cooled cake. Serve with crème fraîche or whipped cream.

Add the dry ingredients to the chocolate mixture.

Beat well to combine the chocolate and dry ingredients.

Pour the mixture into a springform cake pan.

orange crème caramel .... serves 6

THE AIM HERE IS TO PRODUCE A SILKY-SMOOTH CUSTARD WITH NO (OR AT LEAST FEW) BUBBLES IN IT. EASIER SAID THAN DONE, AND GENERALLY PRACTICE IS THE BEST SOLUTION. GET TO KNOW YOUR OVEN AND NOTE WHAT HAPPENS, HAVING THE OVEN TOO HOT OR COOKING FOR TOO LONG CAN LEAD TO ROGUE AIR BUBBLES FORMING.

oranges	4 small
milk	1 cup
light cream	1 cup
vanilla bean	1, split lengthwise
eggs	3, at room temperature
egg yolks	2, at room temperature
superfine sugar	1/2 cup

caramel

superfine sugar	1 1/2 cups

Preheat the oven to 315°F and half-fill a large roasting pan with water. Place the roasting pan in the oven.

Grate the zest of two of the oranges, then peel all the oranges, removing the rind and all the pith. Cut each orange into six slices, discarding any seeds, and place in a flat, heatproof dish.

To make the caramel, put the sugar and 3/4 cup water in a small saucepan over medium heat. Stir constantly for 5 minutes, or until the sugar has completely dissolved. Brush any undissolved sugar from the side of the saucepan with a wet pastry brush. When the sugar has dissolved, increase the heat and boil, without stirring, for 6–7 minutes, or until the mixture has turned golden brown.

Pour the caramel into the base of six 3/4-cup ovenproof ramekins, reserving about 1/2 cup of the caramel. Quickly but carefully stir 1 tablespoon of water into the reserved caramel and pour over the sliced oranges. Cover and refrigerate the oranges.

Put the milk, cream, vanilla bean, and orange zest in a saucepan. Slowly bring to a boil, then remove from heat and set aside to infuse for 10 minutes. Beat the eggs, egg yolks, and sugar in a bowl with an electric beater for 2–3 minutes, or until pale and creamy. Strain the milk mixture over the egg mixture and beat until smooth. Pour the mixture into the ramekins containing the caramel. Put the ramekins into the roasting pan of water and bake for 45 minutes, or until a knife inserted into the center comes out clean. Cover the ramekins with foil if the surface is browning too quickly, making sure the foil doesn't touch the surface. Remove the ramekins from the roasting pan and set aside to cool, then cover and refrigerate for several hours, or overnight.

Remove the crème caramels and oranges from the refrigerator 30 minutes before serving. Unmold the crème caramels onto plates and serve with the oranges.

white chocolate torte

WHAT AN INGREDIENT LIST—EGGS, SUGAR, CHOCOLATE, FLOUR, CREAM, MORE CHOCOLATE, AND MASCARPONE CHEESE! THIS CAKE IS A VERY SIMPLE ONE TO PREPARE, BUT RICH. SERVE A SLICE WITH STRONG COFFEE AND SOME FRESH WINTER FRUIT.

eggs	3, at room temperature
superfine sugar	1/3 cup
white chocolate	1/2 cup chopped, melted
all-purpose flour	1/2 cup, sifted
white chocolate curls	to serve

topping

heavy whipping cream	scant 2/3 cup
white chocolate	1 2/3 cups chopped
mascarpone cheese	scant 2/3 cup

Preheat the oven to 350°F and grease an 8-inch springform cake pan.

Beat the eggs and sugar with an electric beater until thick and pale. Fold in the melted white chocolate and sifted flour. Pour into the prepared pan and bake for 20 minutes, or until a skewer inserted into the center of the cake comes out clean. Set aside in the pan to cool completely.

To make the topping, put the cream and white chocolate in a saucepan. Stir constantly over low heat for 5–6 minutes, or until the chocolate has melted and the mixture is smooth. Remove from heat and set aside to cool slightly. Stir the mascarpone into the chocolate mixture.

Remove the cake from the pan and use a spatula to spread the topping over the top and side. Refrigerate overnight, or until the topping is firm. Serve topped with the chocolate curls.

The process needed to transform the cacao bean (cocoa in English) into that delicious end result known as chocolate is long and complicated, and the block of chocolate, so ubiquitous now, was not perfected until the 1840s. The beans are fermented, dried, and roasted, and the exposed nibs are ground with water to make chocolate liquor. From this comes cocoa butter, as well as a paste that can be dried to make cocoa powder. It is cocoa butter, combined with ground beans and other ingredients such as sugar, that produces chocolate. White chocolate is made from cocoa butter and milk solids, although it differs from milk and bittersweet chocolate in that it does not contain chocolate liquor.

honey parfait with
caramelized kumquats .... serves 6

GOLDEN KUMQUATS, LOOKING LIKE MINIATURE ORANGES, HAVE A FLAVOR THAT IS BOTH SWEET AND TART AT THE SAME TIME. THE ENTIRE FRUIT IS EDIBLE, SO THERE IS NO NEED TO PEEL THEM FOR COOKING. THIS IS FORTUNATE, BECAUSE IT IS ACTUALLY THE SKIN THAT PROVIDES THE SWEETNESS, NOT THE FLESH.

honey	1/4 cup
egg yolks	4, at room temperature
light cream	1 1/4 cups, whipped to soft peaks
orange liqueur, such as Grand Marnier	1 tablespoon
kumquats	12
superfine sugar	1 1/2 cups

Put the honey in a small saucepan and bring to a boil. Beat the egg yolks in a bowl until thick and pale, then add the honey in a slow stream, beating constantly. Gently fold in the cream and liqueur. Pour the mixture into six 1/2-cup freezer-proof molds. Freeze for 4 hours, or until firm.

Wash the kumquats and prick the skins with a skewer. Place the kumquats in a large saucepan, cover with boiling water, and simmer for 20 minutes. Strain the kumquats and reserve 2 cups of the liquid. Return the liquid to the saucepan, add the sugar, and stir over medium heat until the sugar has dissolved. Increase the heat and boil for 10 minutes. Add the kumquats and simmer for 20 minutes, or until the kumquats are soft and the skins are smooth and shiny. Remove from heat and set aside to cool. Lift the kumquats out of the syrup, reserving the syrup.

To serve, dip the molds in hot water for 5–10 seconds before inverting the parfaits onto serving plates. Serve with the caramelized kumquats and a little of the syrup spooned over the top.

Add the boiled honey to the egg yolks, beating constantly.

Prick the skins of the kumquats with a skewer.

Simmer the kumquats until the skins are smooth and shiny.

baked chocolate puddings
with rich chocolate sauce . . . . serves 6

THESE PUDDINGS ONLY TAKE AROUND 10 MINUTES TO COOK AND SHOULD BE SERVED IMMEDIATELY SO THAT THEIR
LUSCIOUS RUNNY CENTERS CAN BE FULLY APPRECIATED. TO ENSURE A SMOOTH DELIVERY TO THE TABLE, HAVE
EVERYTHING ABSOLUTELY READY BEFORE YOU BEGIN.

cocoa powder	1 1/2 tablespoons
good-quality bittersweet chocolate	heaping 3/4 cup chopped
unsalted butter	1/2 cup, softened
eggs	3, at room temperature
egg yolks	2, at room temperature
superfine sugar	1/4 cup
all-purpose flour	3/4 cup

chocolate sauce

good-quality bittersweet chocolate	1/2 cup chopped
light cream	1/2 cup

Preheat the oven to 350°F and grease six 1/2-cup metal dariole molds. Dust the molds with the cocoa powder.

Put the chocolate in a small heatproof bowl over a small saucepan of simmering water, making sure the base of the bowl doesn't touch the water. Allow the chocolate to melt, then add the butter. When the butter has melted, stir to combine, then remove from the heat.

Beat the eggs, egg yolks, and sugar in a large bowl with an electric beater until thick, creamy, and pale in color. Gently fold in the chocolate mixture. Sift in the flour and gently fold through.

Spoon the mixture into the prepared molds, leaving about 1/2 inch at the top of the molds to allow the puddings to rise. Bake for 10 minutes, or until the top is firm and risen.

Meanwhile, to make the chocolate sauce, put the chocolate and cream in a small heatproof bowl and melt over a small saucepan of simmering water, making sure the base of the bowl doesn't touch the water. Stir until combined.

To serve, run a knife around the molds to loosen the puddings, then carefully turn out onto serving plates. Drizzle with the sauce and serve immediately.

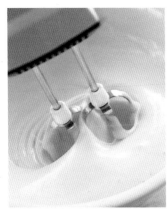

Beat the sugar and eggs until
thick and creamy.

Fold the melted chocolate into
the sugar and egg mixture.

three ways with hot sauces

A SAUCE IS DEFINED AS A SPOONABLE CONCOCTION, AND THESE YUMMY SAUCES WILL CERTAINLY HAVE YOU READY WITH SPOON IN HAND. TRADITIONALLY, SAUCES ARE USED TO ENHANCE THE FLAVORS OF THE FOODS THEY ACCOMPANY, BUT THE ONES GIVEN HERE DISTINGUISH THEMSELVES IN THEIR OWN RIGHT: THE FIRST VIBRANTLY COLORED AND SWEET, THE NEXT RICH AND SMOOTH, AND THE THIRD GENTLY AROMATIC AND MELLOW. ALL ARE AN EASY WAY OF TRANSFORMING INGREDIENTS LIKE FRESH FRUIT AND ICE CREAM INTO A FABULOUS DESSERT.

blood-orange and cardamom sauce

Grate the zest of 2 blood oranges and juice them both. Combine 1 cup water with a heaping 1 cup sugar in a saucepan and stir constantly over medium heat until the sugar has dissolved. Add the orange zest and juice and 5 lightly crushed cardamom pods. Bring to a boil, then reduce the heat to low and simmer for 10 minutes, or until the sauce is a little syrupy. Serve warm. This sauce is delicious poured over steamed puddings, crepes, cakes, or fresh fruit salad. Makes 1¼ cups.

chocolate and baileys sauce

Put ²/₃ cup chopped good-quality bittersweet chocolate, 2 tablespoons unsalted butter, ¼ cup Irish cream liqueur, such as Baileys, and ³/₄ cup heavy whipping cream in a heatproof bowl. Place the bowl over a saucepan of barely simmering water, making sure the base of the bowl doesn't touch the water. Heat until the chocolate has melted. Remove from the heat and stir well to combine. This is great poured over strawberries, ice cream, or cheesecakes. Makes 1½ cups.

cinnamon and pear sauce

Peel, core, and chop 3 just underripe pears and place in a saucepan with 1½ cups water, 1 cup superfine sugar, the juice of ½ lemon, and 2 cinnamon sticks. Bring to a boil, then reduce the heat and simmer for 10 minutes, or until the pears are soft. Remove the cinnamon sticks. Puree the sauce in a blender until smooth. Serve warm. This sauce is great poured over ice cream, fresh fruit, or steamed puddings. Makes 3 cups.

blood orange and cardamom sauce

coconut rice pudding with spiced saffron apples

THIS CREAMY DESSERT WITH ITS DELICATELY SCENTED APPLE TOPPING SHOULD CONVINCE ALL DOUBTERS OF THE MERITS OF RICE PUDDING. APPLES ARE NOT OFTEN PAIRED WITH COCONUT OR RICE, BUT INFUSING THEM WITH THE AROMATIC QUALITIES OF CINNAMON AND SAFFRON TRANSPORTS THEM FROM THE ORCHARD TO THE TROPICS.

short-grain rice	2/3 cup
milk	1 cup
unsweetened light coconut cream	heaping 1 cup
unsalted butter	1 1/2 tablespoons
superfine sugar	2 1/2 tablespoons

saffron apples

red apples	3 small
apple juice	3/4 cup
cinnamon stick	1
saffron threads	pinch
soft brown sugar	1/4 cup

Put the rice, milk, coconut cream, and a scant 1/2 cup of water in a heavy-based saucepan over low–medium heat. Bring to a boil, then reduce heat and simmer, stirring often to prevent the rice from sticking, for 15–20 minutes, or until the mixture is creamy. Beat in the butter and sugar.

Meanwhile, to make the saffron apples, halve and core the apples, then cut into slices. Put the sliced apples, apple juice, cinnamon stick, saffron threads, and brown sugar in a saucepan over low–medium heat. Bring to a boil, then reduce the heat and simmer for 8 minutes, or until the apple is soft.

Serve the rice pudding warm, topped with the saffron apples and their syrup.

Delicious raw or cooked, versatile and amenable to many other flavors, apples are for many the first choice among fruit. They have been cultivated for hundreds of years and exist in many thousands of varieties. It's easy to forget that these everyday companions are seasonal, with most varieties at their peak from autumn to winter. Good eating apples are sweet and often only slightly acidic. They are also perfect for use in pies, since their high sugar content means they will hold their shape well. The more acidic, tart apples become soft when stewed or baked and are ideal for purees and crumbles.

apple galettes . . . . serves 4

AS WITH MANY CLASSIC PIES, THE BEAUTY OF THIS DESSERT LIES IN ITS SIMPLICITY—WARM, PUFFED PASTRY, SWEET FRUIT, AND CARAMELIZED, SLIGHTLY CRUNCHY TOPPING. MAKE YOUR OWN VANILLA SUGAR BY BURYING WHOLE BEANS IN A JAR OF SUGAR. SEAL WELL AND ALLOW 2 TO 3 WEEKS FOR THE VANILLA TO INFUSE THE SUGAR.

ground almonds	1/3 cup
unsalted butter	1 1/2 tablespoons, melted
butter puff pastry	2 sheets, frozen
egg yolk	1, at room temperature, sieved
pink lady apple	1
Granny Smith apple	1
apricot jam	2 tablespoons, warmed and sieved
vanilla sugar	1 tablespoon
heavy cream	to serve

Preheat the oven to 400°F.

Combine the ground almonds and melted butter in a small bowl. Place one sheet of frozen pastry on a sheet of baking paper and lay the second sheet of pastry on top. Cut the pastry into four squares, cutting through the two layers of pastry. (This may be easier when the pastry has thawed slightly but is not too soft.) Slide the baking paper and pastry onto a cookie sheet.

Brush the pastry squares with the sieved egg yolk. Divide the almond mixture among the pastry and spread in a thin layer, leaving the border free.

Thinly slice the apples and alternate the red and green apple slices on each pastry square. Brush with the apricot jam and sprinkle with the vanilla sugar.

Bake the galettes for 15 minutes, or until puffed and golden. Serve warm with heavy cream.

Brush each square of pastry with sieved egg yolk.

Spread the almond mixture onto each pastry square.

Alternate the red and green apple slices.

chocolate, hazelnut, and orange dessert cake with blood-orange sauce . . . . serves 6–8

THIS IS A LOVELY MOIST CAKE, NICELY COMPLEMENTED BY THE CITRUS SAUCE. BLOOD ORANGES HAVE ONLY A SHORT SEASON, SO GRAB THEM WHEN YOU CAN. THEY ARE RICH, SWEET, AND AROMATIC, WITH BOLD RED PIGMENTATION IN THE FLESH AND SKIN. YOU WILL NEED FOUR TO FIVE BLOOD ORANGES FOR THE SYRUP.

good-quality bittersweet chocolate	1 1/3 cups chopped
blanched hazelnuts	1 1/2 cups
unsalted butter	heaping 3/4 cup, softened
raw superfine sugar	3/4 cup
eggs	4, at room temperature, separated
espresso instant coffee granules	3 teaspoons
orange	1, zest finely grated
cornstarch	heaping 3/4 cup
confectioners' sugar	for dusting
heavy cream	to serve

blood-orange syrup

blood-orange juice	1 cup, strained
superfine sugar	1/4 cup
orange liqueur, such as Cointreau	1 teaspoon, optional

Preheat the oven to 325°F and grease an 8-inch springform cake pan.

Put the chocolate in a heatproof bowl and place the bowl over a saucepan of simmering water, making sure the base of the bowl doesn't touch the water. Heat until melted.

Put the hazelnuts in a food processor and process until finely chopped. Cream the butter and superfine sugar in a large bowl with an electric beater until pale and fluffy. Add the egg yolks, one at a time, beating well after each addition. Gently stir in the melted chocolate, coffee granules, and orange zest. Mix in the cornstarch and chopped hazelnuts.

Whisk the egg whites until soft peaks form. Using a large metal spoon, fold a scoop of egg whites into the chocolate mixture. Gently fold in the remaining egg whites. Spoon the mixture into the prepared pan and level the surface. Bake for 30 minutes, then cover loosely with foil and bake for another 40–45 minutes, or until a skewer inserted into the center of the cake comes out clean. Don't be too concerned if the surface cracks.

Meanwhile, to make the blood-orange syrup, pour the strained orange juice into a small saucepan and add the sugar. Stir over low heat until the sugar has dissolved. Bring to a boil, then reduce the heat and simmer for 10–12 minutes, or until reduced by half. Stir in the liqueur, if using, and set aside to cool slightly.

To serve, cut the warm cake into slices. Lightly dust with confectioners' sugar, spoon over a little of the warm orange syrup, and serve with heavy cream.

Add the chopped hazelnuts to the cake mixture.

Simmer the blood-orange juice and sugar together.

brioche with caramelized apples and crème anglaise

THIS IS A FAIRLY INDULGENT DISH, BUT IT IS TEMPTING TO SERVE IT FOR BREAKFAST ON ONE DECADENT DAY. JUST FOCUS ON THE FRUIT AS THE HEALTHY PART. CRÈME ANGLAISE NEEDS TO BE CLOSELY WATCHED DURING COOKING, SINCE IT CAN EASILY CURDLE IF IT GETS TOO HOT.

crème anglaise

egg yolks	4, at room temperature
superfine sugar	1/4 cup
milk	2/3 cup
light cream	2/3 cup
vanilla bean	1, split lengthwise

caramelized apples

Granny Smith apples	3
superfine sugar	1/2 cup
unsalted butter	1 1/2 tablespoons

brioche	six 3/4-inch thick slices
light cream	3/4 cup
eggs	2, at room temperature
orange liqueur, such as Cointreau	2 tablespoons
superfine sugar	2 teaspoons
unsalted butter	2 tablespoons
confectioners' sugar	for dusting

To make the crème anglaise, beat the egg yolks and sugar until just combined. Heat the milk, cream, and vanilla bean in a saucepan until almost boiling. Remove from heat and remove the vanilla bean, scraping the seeds into the liquid. Pour the hot milk mixture onto the egg yolk mixture, mixing well.

Strain the mixture back into a clean saucepan. Stir constantly with a wooden spoon over low heat until the custard has thickened. Do not allow the custard to boil, or it will curdle. Test the consistency by dipping the spoon into the custard and drawing your finger through it—it should leave a clean line. Pour the custard into a bowl, cover, and refrigerate until cold.

To make the caramelized apples, peel and core the apples and cut each into eight wedges. Sprinkle some of the sugar over the base of a heavy-based frying pan and heat gently until the sugar has melted. Sprinkle the remaining sugar into the pan and stir until lightly golden. Add the butter and stir until melted. Add the apples and cook over high heat, gently stirring from time to time, for 10 minutes, or until the apples are well browned. Take care not to overcook the apples—they should still hold their shape. The sugar and butter may separate but will come back together while the apples are cooking. Remove the pan from heat and keep warm.

Cut each brioche slice into a 3 1/2-inch round. Combine the cream, eggs, liqueur, and sugar in a bowl. Melt the butter in a large frying pan over medium heat. Dip the brioche into the egg mixture, allowing it to soak in slightly, then fry until golden brown on both sides. Remove from pan and keep warm.

To serve, pour a portion of cold crème anglaise on a serving plate, top with a round of brioche, and spoon the caramelized apple onto the brioche. Dust lightly with confectioners' sugar.

Use a cookie cutter to cut rounds from the brioche slices.

Allow each brioche round to soak up some of the egg mixture.

pear and walnut frangipane pie .... serves 6–8

FRANGIPANE IS TRADITIONALLY MADE WITH ALMONDS, BUT THIS WALNUT VERSION WORKS PARTICULARLY WELL WITH PEARS. IT WILL RISE SLIGHTLY AS IT COOKS, SURROUNDING THE FRUIT AND HOLDING IT IN PLACE. FRANGIPANE GOES WITH A WHOLE ARRAY OF FRUIT, SO IS AN EXCELLENT BASIC RECIPE TO HAVE IN YOUR REPERTOIRE.

pastry

all-purpose flour	1 1/3 cups
salt	pinch
unsalted butter	1/3 cup, chilled and cubed
egg	1, at room temperature
ice water	2–3 tablespoons
lemon juice	3 teaspoons
pears	3
cinnamon	1/2 teaspoon
superfine sugar	2 tablespoons
vanilla bean	1, split lengthwise
confectioners' sugar	for dusting

walnut frangipane

unsalted butter	heaping 1/3 cup, softened
superfine sugar	1/2 cup
natural vanilla extract	1 teaspoon
eggs	2, at room temperature
ground walnuts	1 1/4 cup
all-purpose flour	1/4 cup

To make the pastry, preheat the oven to 375°F. Lightly grease a 9-inch fluted pie pan. Sift the flour and pinch of salt into a bowl. Combine the butter into the flour using fingertips until the mixture resembles bread crumbs. Beat the egg, half the water, and the lemon juice together in a small bowl, then sprinkle evenly over the flour mixture. Stir with a flat-bladed knife to form a dough, adding the remaining water if necessary. Knead the dough a couple of times on a lightly floured surface. Flatten into a disk, wrap in plastic, and refrigerate for 1 hour.

Peel, core, and slice the pears. Put the pears, cinnamon, and sugar in a saucepan. Scrape the seeds from the vanilla bean into the saucepan and add the pod. Add 1/4 cup water and heat until simmering, then cook for 8 minutes, or until the pear is soft. Set aside.

To make the walnut frangipane, beat the butter and sugar until light and creamy. Add the vanilla and the eggs, one at a time, beating well after each addition. Fold in the ground walnuts and flour until combined.

Roll out the pastry between two sheets of baking paper to line the prepared pan. Carefully place the pastry in the pan, removing the baking paper, and trim any excess pastry. Lightly prick the base with a fork. Refrigerate for 10 minutes.

Line the pastry shell with a sheet of crumpled baking paper and pour in some baking beads or uncooked rice. Bake for 15 minutes, remove the paper and beads, and return to the oven for another 5–8 minutes, or until slightly golden.

Spread the walnut frangipane into the pastry shell and arrange the pear slices on top. Bake for 30–35 minutes, or until the top is lightly browned and the frangipane is firm when tested with a skewer. Serve dusted with confectioners' sugar.

Make sure the frangipane mixture is well combined.

Add a little water to help soften the pears.

chocolate and cinnamon self-saucing puddings

serves 4

THESE INDIVIDUAL PUDDINGS ARE A GREAT WAY TO END A MEAL, AND ALTHOUGH ALL THE WORK NEEDS TO BE DONE ON THE SPOT, THAT SHOULD ONLY TAKE ABOUT 30 MINUTES. THEN, JUST 40 MINUTES IN THE OVEN BEFORE YOU ARE SERVING UP SOME VERY GOOEY, VERY NICE, RICH PUDDINGS.

good-quality bittersweet chocolate	1/3 cup chopped
unsalted butter	1/4 cup, cubed
cocoa powder	2 tablespoons, sifted
milk	2/3 cup
self-rising flour	1 cup
superfine sugar	1/2 cup
soft brown sugar	1/3 cup firmly packed
egg	1, at room temperature, lightly beaten
heavy cream	to serve

cinnamon sauce

ground cinnamon	1 1/2 teaspoons
unsalted butter	1/4 cup, cubed
soft brown sugar	1/3 cup
cocoa powder	1/4 cup, sifted

Preheat the oven to 350°F and grease four 1-cup ovenproof dishes.

Combine the chocolate, butter, cocoa, and milk in a saucepan. Stir over low heat until the chocolate has melted. Remove from the heat.

Sift the flour into a large bowl and stir in the sugars. Add to the chocolate mixture with the egg and mix well. Spoon the mixture into the prepared dishes, put on a baking sheet, and set aside.

To make the cinnamon sauce, put 1 1/2 cups water in a small saucepan. Add the cinnamon, butter, brown sugar, and cocoa, and stir over low heat until combined.

Pour the sauce onto the puddings over the back of a spoon. Bake for 40 minutes, or until firm. Turn out the puddings and serve with heavy cream.

It seems every spice worth the name is difficult to harvest and has been prized and bitterly fought over in equal measure. Cinnamon is no exception. Its use dates back to ancient Egyptian times, when it was used as an embalming agent, and more recently, battles have been fought for its control in its native Sri Lanka. During harvesting, the inner bark is pulled away from the tree *Cinnamomum zeylanicum*, cleaned, dried, and sold as quills or sticks. Cassia bark is often sold as cinnamon, though it does not have the same fine qualities. Cinnamon is also available ground.

tiramisu ice cream..serves 6–8

TIRAMISU MEANS "PICK ME UP" IN ITALIAN, AND THIS SUMPTUOUS ICE CREAM WILL DO JUST THAT. MARSALA IS A FORTIFIED WINE FROM SICILY, AGED FOR 2 TO 5 YEARS. IT HAS A RICH, SMOKY FLAVOR AND A DARK AMBER COLOR. LOOK FOR MARSALA FROM ITALY.

milk	1 cup
vanilla bean	1, split lengthwise
egg yolks	4, at room temperature
superfine sugar	2/3 cup
instant coffee granules	1/3 cup
sweet Marsala	1/3 cup
coffee liqueur	2 tablespoons
boiling water	1/2 cup
heavy whipping cream	1 1/4 cups
ladyfingers	6

Pour the milk into a saucepan. Scrape the seeds from the vanilla bean into the pan and add the pod. Heat slowly for 4–5 minutes, or until just below the boiling point. Discard the vanilla pod. Beat the egg yolks and sugar with an electric beater until pale and frothy. Gradually pour the hot milk mixture over the egg mixture and beat until smooth. Return the mixture to the saucepan and stir constantly over low heat for 6–8 minutes, or until the custard has thickened and coats the back of a spoon.

Remove the pan from heat. Strain the custard and divide it between two freezer-proof bowls. Dissolve half the coffee granules in one bowl and stir the Marsala into the other. Refrigerate both bowls of custard for 30 minutes.

Combine the remaining coffee granules, the coffee liqueur, and boiling water in a small bowl. Refrigerate until required.

Whip the cream until soft peaks form. Fold half the cream through the coffee custard and half through the Marsala custard. Transfer the bowls to the freezer. When the ice cream starts to set, whisk well with an electric beater to break up the ice crystals. Return to the freezer until the ice cream is firm again, then beat well.

Line the base and the two long sides of a 5 1/2 x 6 1/2-inch, 2 1/2-inch-deep loaf pan with foil and brush with water. Spoon the coffee ice cream into the pan, leveling the surface. Dip both sides of the ladyfingers in the chilled coffee liqueur mixture and arrange over the coffee ice cream in a tight layer, trimming to fit, and gently pressing them down. Spoon the Marsala ice cream over the top and level the surface. Cover the pan with foil and freeze until set. Lift out of the pan, remove the foil, and cut into slices to serve.

Alternatively, to prepare the ice cream in an ice-cream machine, churn the coffee custard until partly set, then spoon into the pan, top with the coffee-soaked ladyfingers, and freeze while you churn the Marsala custard.

Soak the ladyfingers in the coffee liqueur mixture.

Cut the ladyfingers to fit snugly in the pan.

the perfect soufflé

Soufflés can be sweet or savory and are held up by beaten egg whites and hot air. Technically, soufflés are always hot, although iced or cold mousses are sometimes referred to as soufflés. A sweet soufflé is based on custard or fruit puree, to which melted chocolate, nuts, fruit, and liqueur can be added. Once a soufflé mixture is made, it must be baked immediately and then served immediately.

To make the perfect chocolate soufflé, preheat the oven to 400°F and put a baking sheet into the oven to preheat. Wrap a double layer of baking paper around six 1-cup ramekins to come 1¼ inches above the rim and secure with string. This encourages the soufflé to rise well. Brush the insides of the ramekins with melted butter and sprinkle with superfine sugar, shaking to coat evenly and tipping out any excess. This layer of butter and sugar helps the soufflé to grip the sides and rise as it cooks.

Put 1¼ cups chopped good-quality bittersweet chocolate in a large heatproof bowl. Place over a saucepan of simmering water, making sure the base of the bowl doesn't touch the water. Stir until the chocolate is melted and smooth, then remove the bowl from the saucepan. Stir 5 lightly beaten egg yolks and ¼ cup superfine sugar into the chocolate. Beat 7 egg whites until firm peaks form. Gently fold one-third of the egg whites into the chocolate mixture to loosen it. Then, using a metal spoon, fold in the remaining egg whites until just combined. Spoon the mixture into the prepared ramekins and run your thumb or a blunt knife around the inside rim of the dish and the edge of the mixture. This ridge helps the soufflé to rise evenly. Place the ramekins on the preheated baking sheet and bake for 12–15 minutes, or until well risen and just set. Do not open the oven door while the soufflés are baking. Cut the string and remove the paper collars. Serve immediately, lightly dusted with sifted confectioners' sugar. Makes 6.

asian pear and rhubarb meringue pie

. . . . serves 6

MOST CHILDREN BLANCH AT RHUBARB. PERHAPS BECAUSE IT LOOKS LIKE A VEGETABLE—AND IS IN FACT BOTANICALLY CLASSIFIED AS SUCH. BUT WITH MATURITY COMES A NEWFOUND APPRECIATION OF THE TENDER PINK STALKS—PARTICULARLY WHEN COOKED WITH JUICY ASIAN PEARS AND SWEET MERINGUE.

unsalted butter	1/4 cup, chilled and cubed
all-purpose flour	1 cup, sifted
superfine sugar	2 tablespoons
salt	1/2 teaspoon
iced water	1 tablespoon
egg yolks	2, at room temperature
natural vanilla extract	1/4 teaspoon

filling

Asian pears	2
rhubarb	5 stalks (about 14 1/2 ounces)
superfine sugar	1/4 cup
vanilla bean	1, split lengthwise
cornstarch	3 teaspoons

meringue

egg whites	3, at room temperature
superfine sugar	1/2 cup
confectioners' sugar	for dusting

To make the pastry, preheat the oven to 350°F. Lightly grease an 8 1/2-inch, 3/4-inch-deep, loose-bottomed fluted pie pan. Combine the butter and flour together in a bowl using fingertips until the mixture resembles bread crumbs. Combine the sugar, salt, water, egg yolks, and vanilla in a separate bowl, then blend into the flour mixture using a flat-bladed knife. Briefly knead the dough on a lightly floured surface until smooth. Flatten into a disk, wrap in plastic, and refrigerate for 30 minutes.

Meanwhile, to make the filling, peel, core, and cut the pears into 3/4-inch pieces. Trim and cut the rhubarb stalks into 1 1/2-inch lengths. Put the pear, sugar, and 1/2 cup water in a saucepan. Scrape the seeds from the vanilla bean into the saucepan and add the pod. Bring to a boil, then stir, reduce the heat, and simmer over low–medium heat for 5 minutes. Add the rhubarb and simmer for 10 minutes, or until the pear and rhubarb are soft. Stir 1 tablespoon of water into the cornstarch until smooth, stir into the rhubarb mixture and cook until thickened. Set aside to cool. Discard the vanilla pod.

Roll out the pastry between two sheets of baking paper to line the prepared pan. Carefully place the pastry in the pan, removing the baking paper, and trim any excess pastry. Lightly prick the base with a fork. Refrigerate for 15 minutes.

Line the pastry shell with a sheet of crumpled baking paper and pour in some baking beads or uncooked rice. Bake for 15 minutes, remove the paper and beads, and return to the oven for another 8 minutes. Set the pastry aside to cool. Increase the oven temperature to 400°F.

To make the meringue, beat the egg whites with an electric beater until soft peaks form. Add the sugar, 1 tablespoon at a time, beating well after each addition until the sugar has dissolved. Continue beating and adding sugar until the meringue is thick and glossy. Spoon the filling into the pastry case, then spoon the meringue on top of the filling and dust with confectioners' sugar. Bake for 8 minutes, or until lightly browned. Serve at room temperature.

Cut the trimmed rhubarb stalks into short lengths.

Use the back of a spoon to make peaks in the meringue.

apple and passion-fruit crumble . . . . serves 4–6

THERE ARE COUNTLESS VERSIONS OF THE FRUIT CRUMBLE, BUT ALL RELY ON THE WINNING FORMULA OF SWEETENED FRUIT COVERED BY A GOLDEN TOPPING OF FLOUR, SUGAR, AND BUTTER. HERE, PASSION FRUIT AND SHREDDED COCONUT ADD A LITTLE COMPLEXITY TO THE BASIC FLAVORS.

passion fruits	4
Granny Smith apples	4
superfine sugar	1/4 cup, plus 1/3 cup
shredded dried coconut	1 cup
all-purpose flour	3/4 cup
unsalted butter	1/3 cup, softened

Preheat the oven to 350° and grease a 4-cup ovenproof dish.

Sieve the passion fruits, discarding the pulp, and place the juice in a bowl. Peel, core, and thinly slice the apples and add to the passion-fruit juice, along with the 1/4 cup of sugar. Mix well, then transfer the mixture to the prepared dish.

Combine the shredded dried coconut, flour, 1/3 cup sugar, and butter in a bowl and rub together until the mixture has a crumble texture. Pile on top of the apple mixture.

Bake the crumble for 25–30 minutes, or until the topping is crisp and golden.

Make sure you squeeze out as much juice as possible.

Peel the apples and cut out all the cores.

Use your fingertips to rub the butter into the dry ingredients.

chocolate orange pots . . . . serves 8

ANYTHING THAT CONTAINS CREAM AND CHOCOLATE AND NOT MUCH ELSE IS GOING TO BE RICH. AND WHILE THE ZEST OF ONE ORANGE WILL NOT DO MUCH TO ALTER THAT, ITS CLEAN, PERFUMED QUALITIES ARE AN ESSENTIAL PART OF THIS DISH. WASH AND DRY THE ORANGE BEFORE GRATING IT, TAKING CARE TO AVOID THE WHITE PITH.

heavy whipping cream	2 cups
good-quality bittersweet chocolate	1²/₃ cups chopped
powdered gelatin	2 teaspoons
egg yolks	6, at room temperature
orange	1, zest finely grated

Heat the cream in a small saucepan until it is just coming to a boil. Add the chocolate and stir over low heat until the chocolate has melted and the mixture is well combined.

Put ¼ cup water in a small bowl and sprinkle with the gelatin. Leave the gelatin to sponge and swell. Stir the gelatin mixture into the hot chocolate mixture.

Beat the egg yolks with an electric beater for 3 minutes, or until thick and pale. Whisk a little of the hot chocolate mixture into the yolks, then pour the yolk mixture onto the remaining chocolate mixture, whisking continuously. Stir in the orange zest.

Divide the mixture among eight ½-cup ramekins and refrigerate overnight to set. Serve the chocolate pots topped with extra orange zest, if desired.

Originating in China, oranges are now a mainstay of many people's daily diet the world over. Oranges have come far from their early days and can be classified along the following lines: blood (vibrant color, rich and sweet); sweet (good juice, some seeds); navel (easy to peel, full of flavor, and nearly always seedless); and bitter Seville (aromatic skin and tart flavor; used in marmalade, in liqueurs, and to make orange-flower water). When buying, choose oranges that feel heavy and have tight skin. The skin of most commercially available oranges is coated with a wax polish. If you are using the zest, scrub the fruit very well first or, better still, buy organic unpolished oranges.

almond and rosewater puddings
with orange and date salad . . . . serves 4

THESE PRETTY PUDDINGS CONTAIN BITTER ALMOND AROMA, WHICH IS AVAILABLE FROM SOME SPECIALITY FOOD STORES. IT IS PREFERABLE TO ALMOND EXTRACT; HOWEVER, 1/4 TEASPOON OF ALMOND EXTRACT CAN BE USED SUCCESSFULLY, IF YOU ARE UNABLE TO LOCATE ALMOND AROMA.

powdered gelatin	3 teaspoons
milk	2 cups
superfine sugar	2 tablespoons
bitter almond aroma	1/2 teaspoon
rose water	1 teaspoon
oranges	2
fresh dates	8, pitted and roughly chopped

Put 1/4 cup water in a small bowl and sprinkle with the gelatin. Leave the gelatin to sponge and swell. Stir the milk and sugar in a small saucepan over medium heat until the sugar has dissolved. When the milk reaches lukewarm, remove the saucepan from heat. Continue stirring while you add the gelatin mixture, and stir until it has dissolved into the warm milk. Strain into a bowl, then stir in the almond aroma and rose water.

Pour the mixture into four 1/2-cup dariole molds and refrigerate for at least 3 hours, or until firm.

Slice the tops and bases off the oranges and place on a board. Use a small sharp knife to cut downward, removing the skin and pith. Holding the oranges over a bowl, remove the segments by slicing in between the membranes. Remove any seeds. Add the segments to the bowl with the juice. Squeeze any remaining juice from the orange skeletons. Add the chopped dates to the bowl and toss to combine.

To serve, wrap the dariole molds in a hot, clean dish towel and invert the puddings onto plates. Accompany the puddings with the orange and date salad.

Strain the warm milk and gelatin mixture into a bowl.

Peel the orange, removing all of the white pith.

Slice in between the membranes, avoiding any white pith.

ricotta, orange, and walnut cake . . . . serves 6–8

THIS CAKE SHOWS JUST HOW MANY FLAVORS ORANGES CAN COMPLEMENT—NUTS, RICOTTA, AND COCOA. AS SUCH, IT NEEDS NO DRESSING UP. BUY THE DRY BULK RICOTTA AVAILABLE FROM DELICATESSENS FOR THIS CAKE; THE SMOOTH RICOTTA SOLD IN PREPACKAGED TUBS IS NOT SUITABLE.

walnut halves	1 1/2 cups
unsalted butter	3/4 cup, softened
superfine sugar	2/3 cup
eggs	5, at room temperature, separated
orange	1 large, zest finely grated
lemon juice	1 teaspoon
ricotta cheese	heaping 3/4 cup
all-purpose flour	1/2 cup
cocoa powder	for dusting

candied orange zest

orange	1 large
boiling water	to cover
orange juice	1 cup
superfine sugar	1/2 cup

Preheat the oven to 400°F and grease an 8 1/2-inch springform cake pan.

Spread the walnuts on a baking sheet and toast for 5 minutes. Use a sharp knife to roughly chop two-thirds of the walnuts. Set aside. Finely chop the remaining walnuts in a food processor and use to coat the inside of the prepared pan in a thick layer. Reduce the oven to 375°F.

Cream the butter and a heaping 1/3 cup of the sugar in a large bowl with an electric beater until pale and fluffy. Add the egg yolks, orange zest, lemon juice, ricotta, flour, and reserved walnuts, and mix gently until well combined.

Whisk the egg whites in a large bowl until soft peaks form. Gradually add the remaining sugar and whisk until stiff. Using a metal spoon, fold a large scoop of the egg-white mixture into the ricotta mixture. Carefully fold in the remaining egg-white mixture. Spoon into the prepared pan and level the surface. Bake for 35–40 minutes, or until the cake is set and the surface is golden. Cool in the pan for 15 minutes before turning out.

Meanwhile, to make the candied orange zest, carefully peel the orange using a sharp paring knife, discarding all the pith. Cut the zest into long strips, 1/8-inch wide. Place the zest in a bowl and cover with boiling water. Set aside to soak for 3–4 minutes, then drain and dry on paper towels. Stir the orange juice and sugar in a small saucepan until the sugar has dissolved. Bring to a boil, then add the orange zest and simmer for 5 minutes. Remove the zest with tongs and spread on a plate to cool.

To serve, dust the center of the cake with cocoa, leaving 2 inches of the rim uncovered. Arrange the orange zest around the rim and serve the cake in slices.

Thinly slice the orange zest into long strips.

Simmer the zest in the sugar syrup for 5 minutes.

index

Thunder Bay Press
An imprint of the Advantage Publishers Group
5880 Oberlin Drive, San Diego, CA 92121-4794
www.thunderbaybooks.com

All notations of errors or omissions should be addressed to Thunder Bay Press, Editorial Department, at the above address. All other correspondence (author inquiries, permissions) concerning the content of this book should be addressed to Murdoch Books Pty Limited, Pier 8/9 23 Hickson Road, Millers Point NSW 2000 Australia.

ISBN-13: 978-1-59223-533-9
ISBN-10: 1-59223-533-6
Library of Congress Cataloging-in-Publication Data available upon request.

Printed by Toppan Printing Hong Kong Co. Ltd. Printed in China.
1 2 3 4 5   09 08 07 06 05

IMPORTANT: Those who might be at risk from the effects of salmonella poisoning (the elderly, pregnant women, young children, and those suffering from immune deficiency diseases) should consult their doctor with any concerns about eating raw eggs.

CONVERSION GUIDE: You may find cooking times vary depending on the oven you are using. For convection ovens, as a general rule, set the oven temperature to 70°F lower than indicated in the recipe.

Chief Executive: Juliet Rogers
Publisher: Kay Scarlett
Design concept and art direction: Vivien Valk
Designer: Annette Fitzgerald
Project manager: Paul McNally
Editor: Justine Harding
Text: Margaret Malone
Food editor: Katy Holder
Recipes: Lee Currie, Ross Dobson, Michelle Earl, Jo Glynn, Katy Holder, Kathy Knudsen, Angela Nahas,
    Fiona Roberts, Mandy Sinclair, Abi Ulgiati
Photographer: Alan Benson
Stylist: Mary Harris
Food preparation: Jo Glynn
Production: Adele Troeger